The

F A M I L Y
. . . . . .

God's
Handiwork

Warmest christian
greetings.

Jim Williams
June 2/84

The Family

GOD'S HANDIWORK

John Williams

LIVING STUDIES
Tyndale House Publishers, Inc.
Wheaton, Illinois

Scripture quotations are from
The Holy Bible, New International Version,
Copyright © 1978
by New York International Bible Society.

First printing, April 1984
Library of Congress Catalog Card Number 83-51425
ISBN 0-8423-0841-5 paper
Copyright © 1984 by John Williams
Printed in the United States of America

Gratefully dedicated to my family,
God's greatest earthly gift to me.

CONTENTS

PAUL'S TEACHING ABOUT MARRIAGE AND FAMILY

SOME CONTEMPORARY APPLICATIONS

PART ONE

MARRIAGE AND FAMILY IN THE OLD TESTAMENT

". . . holy Matrimony: which is an honourable estate, instituted by God in the time of man's innocency, signifying unto us the mystical union that is betwixt Christ and his Church; . . . it was ordained for the procreation of children . . . for a remedy against sin . . . for mutual society, help and comfort."

> (The form of Solemnization of Matrimony,
> The Book of Common Prayer, 1571)

CHAPTER ONE

MARRIAGE
IN THE BEGINNING

Marriage was instituted by God and is to be carefully cultivated and protected. It is both the purpose and fulfillment of our human sexuality, and the proper context of family life and happiness. There are few more beautiful lines about marriage than these taken from Genesis: "Then the Lord God made a woman. . . . and he brought her to the man. The man said, This is now bone of my bones and flesh of my flesh" (Genesis 2:22, 23).

As we examine certain Bible stories we sometimes read about marriage failure, but these failures are always recognized for what they are—deviations from the divine intention. If we insist on applying the New Testament criteria for Christian marriage to the Old Testament stories we will be disappointed. But we can see that Old Testament patterns and principles still have much to teach us about how to build and foster meaningful relationships and happy homes. This is clear from the fact that both Jesus and Paul build their teaching about marriage and family on the basis of God's order in creation (Matthew 19:4, 5; Ephesians 5:31).

IN THE IMAGE OF GOD

"Then God said, 'Let us make man in our image, in our likeness, and let them rule over the fish of the sea and the birds of the air, over the livestock, over all the earth, and over all the creatures that move along the ground.' So God created man in his own image, in the image of God he created him; male and female he created them" (Genesis 1:26, 27).

The Bible thus presents man as a creature of God, and interprets all human relationships, including marriage and family, in the light of this premise. In fact, only if we understand the teaching of the book of Genesis will we be able to build a biblical view of marriage.

When we read that man was created in the "image and likeness of God" we must understand that this is not some kind of reverse anthropomorphism. The writer is not suggesting that man is some sort of demigod. Genesis is not mythology but a serious attempt to explain that man is unique compared with all the other creatures God had made.

In fact, the Bible is not concerned so much with the creation of the physical—shall we say material— side of man as with his personhood and real being. This explains the nonsense we hear about the "unscientific nature of the biblical story of origins." Genesis is not really concerned with methods or processes of creation but with the fact that while man bears a physical relationship to the rest of creation, he is a unique being. His significance and value can be appreciated only if we see him as bearing the image of an intelligent, infinite Creator. *When* God created man, or *how* he created him, is not important to biblical writers. They are more concerned with *why;* that is to say, with the purpose and nature of man.

Man in the image of God is a personal, rational, responsible, creative, sovereign, and spiritual creature. He is capable of moral choice and intelligent decision; but also (and this is essential to marriage) capable of deep and meaningful relationships. Of course, while man has these marvelous capabilities—he does not have complete control of them, and thus is often frustrated. This is what the Bible calls "sin," and what we call human depravity. Such a doctrine does not lead to despair but to hope. However, it does cut man down to size and challenges him to turn in trusting obedience back to his Creator. It is in this returning that man discovers not only his full potential but also new freedom—as well as new dimensions in relationships with other human beings.

MAN AS MALE AND FEMALE

"When God created man, he made him in the likeness of God. He created them male and female; at the time they were created, he blessed them and called them 'man'" (Genesis 5:1, 2).

When we use the word "man" we tend to limit it to the masculine gender. In the Genesis story, in the verses cited above, the words "man" or "Adam" represent both genders. Maleness and femaleness are complementary expressions of the one whole that is man as created in God's image.

In Genesis chapter one the creation story is theocentric (God-centered) and generalized. In chapter two it is anthropocentric (man-centered) and detailed. There is no contradiction between these chapters, as some casual readers suggest. Chapter one presents the broad sweep of the creation with man as its crown. Chapter two focuses in on man in relation to: God (v. 7), his environment (vv. 9-14), his responsibility (vv. 15-17), his sovereignty (vv. 19, 20) (Genesis 1:26; Psalm 8), and finally, his sexuality (vv. 18, 20-24).

This matter of human sexuality is important for our present study. Several things surface in the beautiful story told in Genesis 2:18-24. First there is God's concern for Adam as a personal being. It is this, in the context of our story, that tells why he created Eve. Second, we see also the relational side of man. Adam as a personal being is seen as lonely and unfulfilled. He stands peerless in creation but in need of a "helpmeet," meaning that if man is to realize his innate capability of relationship, he needs someone to relate to; or as the Bible puts it, he needs "a helper suitable for him" (2:18). This need is a further evidence that man was created in God's image. The God of the Bible is not an impersonal, passionless, independent being but a live person who enjoys and expresses himself in relationships.

Third, the sovereignty of God is shown in this story as well as the response of Adam. God created Eve quite independently of man; but man immediately responded to her, seeing her as intrinsically herself and yet of himself. It is as though he looked in a mirror and liked what he saw, realizing that the image was alive. It is as though he said: "She is me;

yet she is not me!" This is even suggested in the Hebrew words for man and woman, *"Ish"* and *"Ishah."*

As we look more closely at this story we learn a great deal about the basis of human relationships. It tells us that God "built" Eve out of Adam. We read: "So the Lord God caused the man to fall into a deep sleep; and while he was sleeping, he took one of the man's ribs and closed up the place with flesh. Then the Lord God made a woman from the rib he had taken out of the man, and he brought her to the man" (Genesis 2:21, 22).

From the lovely imagery of this story we learn several things. First, man had nothing to do with the creation of woman. She was God's handiwork. It is almost as though the narrator is stressing this when he tells us that the man was asleep. It was not simply a matter of anesthesia; it was perhaps to make sure he did not interfere!

Second, while woman is independent of man, she is a part of him. Whether the writer intends us to think of a rib in the literal sense is unimportant. It is relationship that is in view. The Hebrew for "rib" is probably better read as "side" (cf. NIV, margin), which might suggest that "woman" is, in fact, one whole side of man's personality. There is a special beauty about femaleness. Yet this distinction is best understood when compared with maleness. Today many people tend to overemphasize and to exploit the physical side of human sexuality. The Bible, while recognizing this physical aspect, seems more concerned in the creation narrative to draw attention to the psychological and spiritual union of a man and his wife.

It is sad, if not libelous, that in the controversy over

sexism in our day, the Bible has been attacked as one of the supporting documents of male chauvinism. Misinformed women's liberationists have seen the Bible as the magna carta of male supremacy and have declared it off limits to all who want to establish women's rights.

The truth is that no other piece of literature has done more to establish the dignity of womanhood and to liberate women from slavery than the Bible. And the particular story we are looking at tells us why. It shows us that woman was created by God not as a kind of toy for a "macho Adam," but as his partner and complement. To use the New Testament phrase, Adam and Eve as husband and wife are seen as "heirs together of the grace of life" (1 Peter 3:7). Augustine, commenting on the Genesis story, noted that God did not build women out of man's head lest she dominate him; nor out of his foot lest he dominate her; but out of his side so that they would be partners.

VIVE LA DIFFERENCE!
Quite apart from man and woman being psychologically complementary, there is their physical diversity. This idea is clearly present in Scripture in the creation story. Sex is not a dirty word in the Bible but part of God's design and purpose for mankind (see Genesis 1:28). It has been well said that God performed the first marriage. As already noted, the simple words of the Bible are, ". . . [God] brought her to the man."

In the miracle of their heterosexuality, and the wonder of their mutual love, man and woman discovered both psychological and physical fulfillment. Here lies the basic pattern for marital relationship. Anything different, be it a homosexual relationship or extramarital sex, is an aberration and is in fact under divine censure and judgment (Exodus 20:14; Deuteronomy 22:2; Leviticus 18:22; 20:13).

The procreation of children is a perfectly natural and expected result of marriage. Children ideally are born of an act of love which also satisfies the sexual desire. Here lies one of the bases of security within both marriage and family. This is part of the meaning of the words: "For this reason a man will leave his father and mother and be united [cleave: KJV] to his wife, and they will become one flesh" (Genesis 2:24).

LEAVING AND CLEAVING

Other important aspects of marriage and family are expressed in the words "leaving" and "cleaving." These words imply a unique and independent role for each generation and each new family unit. Once children reach adulthood it is natural and to be expected that they will leave the family nest and go forth to establish their own families and homes. Each new family is not merely a surrogate but a new, independent, and responsible family under God.

These words also imply a responsibility to understand that only as people properly "leave" can they responsibly "cleave." This means that parents are responsible to prepare their offspring for marriage; and when marriage comes, to allow their parent-child ties to be severed. It also suggests that the new couple now joined together must accept responsibility and conscientiously establish a new family unit. Young marrieds who feel threatened should see that while the "cleaving" requires "leaving," the "cleaving" more than compensates for the "leaving"!

The word *cleave* suggests the permanence of the marriage relationship. More will be said of this later, but the Genesis story clearly implies monogamy, fidelity, and permanence, at the very minimum.

Something must be said about the effects of the "Fall of Man," mentioned in Genesis. Whatever else was lost in the Fall, human sexuality survived. Sexuality was changed, and evidently bounded by new limits; but it was still a part of man the sinner. We are not going to study the theology of the Fall of man, but it is clear that the Fall brought about changes in human relationships and family life.

Some of the warmth of Adam and Eve's mutual trust must have evaporated after the Fall. After all, Adam's laying the blame on Eve for his own failure would do nothing to encourage her confidence in him, just as Eve's deception by Satan must have eroded some of Adam's confidence in her (Genesis 3:10-13). They must have seen a moral need to provide some covering for their nakedness. With the development of these feelings of personal embarrassment came an uneasiness in the presence of God.

Although Genesis tells us that God held our first parents accountable and punished them for their sin, it also shows us that he tempers his judgment with mercy. The punishment involved a number of things. For example, the pleasure of the procreative process was to be mingled with pain just as the pleasure of work was to be blurred by toil. Further, instead of the freedom and equality of Adam and Eve's spotless partnership, they came to know domination and subjection. Man now reproduced in his own likeness and image (see Genesis 5:3); and the image of God in man, though not obliterated, was badly defaced. Despite their failure and disobedience, God still cared for them. In the so-called protevangelium of Genesis 3:15, he even declared that they would still be his instruments in the ultimate plan of salvation.

Without getting ahead of our story—how grateful we are to see the fulfillment of God's promise in the New Testament! There we see men and women redeemed by Christ and restored not only to relationship with God but also to each other. In Christ man regains his liberty and a sense of dignity in work, while woman receives the promised blessing of God at childbirth (Colossians 3:17; 1 Timothy 2:15). But more of this later! Meanwhile, let Charles Wesley say it for us:

> *Come Desire of Nations come!*
> *Fix in us thy humble home:*
> *Rise, the women's conquering seed,*
> *Bruise in us the Serpent's head.*
> *Adam's likeness now efface,*
> *Stamp thine image in its place:*
> *Second Adam from above*
> *Reinstate us in Thy love.*
> (Charles Wesley, 1707-1788)

STUDY QUESTIONS

1. How do you understand the idea: "man created in the image of God"?

2. In what ways does this biblical view of man dignify humanity and guarantee freedom?

3. Consider ways in which man and woman (as male and female) complement each other.

4. How do you understand "helpmeet" in Genesis 2:18?

5. What do you consider to be the basic purposes of marriage?

6. What things should be carefully discussed by a couple intending to be married?

7. What are the "limits of marriage" suggested in the creation story?

8. Why is a "wedding occasion" desirable?

9. Suggest a set of wedding vows.

10. Consider the sad consequences of the Fall.

MARRIAGE IN OLD TESTAMENT TIMES

While there is no particular Old Testament passage which deals comprehensively with the subject of marriage, this first part of our Bible offers all kinds of information and counsel. As we examine these Old Testament passages we must bear in mind that we are not only looking at ancient marital traditions, but we are seeing them in a culture quite different from our own. We must seek to see what is cultural and historical and what is ethical and abiding.

ARRANGED MARRIAGES

One of the first things to strike the Westerner as he reads about Old Testament marriages is that the parents had the responsibility of finding suitable partners for their children. Apparently such arrangements might be made quite early, while children were still young, with the actual marriage taking place when the parties reached their early teens. The Jews tended to marry young. Girls could marry at twelve and boys when they were thirteen. The idea was that it was better for a person to marry at puberty and thus be safeguarded against promiscuity.

One of the well-known arranged marriages of the Old Testament was between Isaac and Rebekah. We hear Abraham saying to his chief servant, "I want you to swear by the Lord, the God of heaven and the God of earth, that you will not get a wife for my son from the daughters of the Canaanites, among whom I am living, but will go to my country and my own relatives and get a wife for my son Isaac" (Genesis 24:3, 4).

As this beautiful tale unfolds we see how the ancient traditions are observed. For example, before any formal arrangements could be made, Rebekah's father and brother (v. 50) had to be consulted and their permission obtained. This done, the servant who had already given Rebekah gold bracelets, formally handed over very costly gifts to her family. Although not specifically stated, this was probably the *Mohar* or "bride price," the money or in-kind-payment usually given to the father. It was partly a compensation for the loss of his daughter and partly a guarantee of her future in the event of her husband's early death (see Genesis 31:14). This custom of the *Mohar* is more obvious in the later story where Laban tricked Jacob into working fourteen years for his daughters Leah and Rachel (Genesis 29:14-30). Finally, there is the bride-to-be's consent (vv. 57, 58), although at this point it seems to be little more than lip service. Other well-known Old Testament examples of arranged marriages include Othniel and Achsah (Joshua 15:16, 17); Samson and the woman of Timnah (Judges 14:1-4); and Ruth and Boaz (book of Ruth).

While this custom of contractual marriage may seem to preclude the possibility of marriage for love, such was evidently not the case. The Old Testament stories (including those already referred to) indicate that the marriages were usually characterized by the enjoyment of love. People evidently learned to love each other and discovered a deep sense of security together. In societies where arranged marriages are still practiced, divorce rates are lower. There may, of course, be other contributing factors.

OLD TESTAMENT ATTITUDE TO MARRIAGE

The Old Testament presents a very positive view of marriage and takes it for granted that this is a normal, God-given relationship. Proverbs 18:22 is typical: "He who finds a wife finds what is good and receives favor from the Lord." One chapter later we read, "Houses and wealth are inherited from parents, but a prudent wife is from the Lord" (Proverbs 19:14). In fact, not to be married was considered something of a disgrace in Old Testament society. We read, for example, "In that day seven women will take hold of one man and say, 'We will eat our own food and provide our own clothes; only let us be called by your name. Take away our disgrace' " (Isaiah 4:1).

The Old Testament is surprisingly frank about marital love. The entire Song of Solomon, whatever its deeper symbolism, is written in praise of love and takes the form of a love song. It includes many quite specific references to the physical aspects of love. The writer, despite his pessimism, recommends: "Enjoy life with your wife, whom you love" (Ecclesiastes 9:9). Proverbs 5:18, 19 says: "May your fountain be blessed, and may you rejoice in the wife of your youth, a loving doe, a graceful deer—may her breasts satisfy you always, may you ever be captivated by her love."

The law made special provision for the newly married bridegroom. He was exempt from military service and other responsibilities. For one year he was to be free to stay at home and bring happiness to the wife he had married. Similarly a man who was betrothed to be married was allowed to return home if battle was imminent. The ruling reads: "Has anyone become pledged to a woman and not married her? Let him go home, or he may die in battle and someone else marry her" (Deuteronomy 20:7).

If marital love is enjoined, so is faithfulness in marriage. Any deviation from this strict moral code was regarded with the utmost seriousness. Adultery was not only forbidden by the Decalogue (Exodus 20:14), but was considered a capital offense under the Levitical code (Leviticus 18:20; Deuteronomy 22:22-24). Some measure of the seriousness of marital unfaithfulness can be seen from the fact that it is used metaphorically of idolatry. Israel is viewed in the Old Testament as Jehovah's wife, and idolatry and apostasy are described as "spiritual fornication" (Isaiah 57:3; Jeremiah 3:8; Ezekiel 23:43). It is this attitude that accounts for the strange story of Hosea. In this book the prophet is commanded to marry "an adulterous wife." He is to do this in order to give a live demonstration (acted parable) of Israel's unfaithfulness to the Lord. "The Lord said to him, 'Go, take to yourself an adulterous wife and children

of unfaithfulness, because the land is guilty of
the vilest adultery in departing from the Lord'"
(Hosea 1:2; 3:1).

MONOGAMY

While the Old Testament recognizes the existence of
polygamy, it is regarded as a deviation from the divine
ideal. Its origin is often traced to Lamech, the
unsavory great great grandson of Cain (Genesis 4:19).
Generally speaking, the ordinary people of Bible times
observed the "one man, one woman" order of
Creation. Only the more well-to-do were able to
practice polygamy. Judging from the Old Testament
story of Solomon, the more affluent, materialistic, and
spiritually obtuse a man became, the more likely he
was to maintain his harem (1 Kings 11:1-6;
Nehemiah 13:26).

The fact that men like Abraham, Jacob, Elkanah,
David, Solomon, and others practiced polygamy in no
way enhances their image in Scripture, nor suggests
that God condoned their actions. In fact, their very
departure from God's will in this matter brought all
kinds of heartache to themselves and to their
posterity. Perhaps the most notorious example, the
results of which still threaten to destroy modern
civilization, was Abraham's "marriage" to Hagar. The
issue of that union was Ishmael, from whom sprang
the Arab nations. There is still no love lost between
the descendants of Isaac and Ishmael.

We have already referred to God's condemnation of
idolatry as "spiritual fornication." That in itself
implies that God's ideal is "one husband, one wife."
The imagery would have been meaningless in the
face of a polygamous marriage ethic.

While polygamy is nowhere condoned in the Old Testament, it is strictly regulated. We read for example: "If a man has two wives, and he loves one but not the other, and both bear him sons but the firstborn is the son of the wife he does not love, when he wills his property to his sons, he must not give the rights of the firstborn to the son of the wife he loves in preference to his actual firstborn. . . . He must acknowledge the son of his unloved wife as the firstborn by giving him a double share of all he has" (Deuteronomy 21:15-17).

We should note another unusual practice of Old Testament times, the so-called levirate marriage. Under this custom a man was expected to marry the widow of his brother. The idea seems to have been to preserve a family name which might otherwise become extinct because the brother had left no male heirs. Furthermore, it guaranteed the preservation of the family property.

Levirate marriage was not inevitable and might be declined. In this case a man might officially refuse to marry his sister-in-law. To do so evidently incurred some disgrace (Deuteronomy 25:7-10). We have an example of this in the story of Boaz and Ruth (Ruth 4:2-7).

RESTRICTIONS REGARDING MARRIAGE
Generally speaking, early Old Testament custom required a man to marry within his own tribal group or clan (Genesis 34:14). This is evident in the stories of Isaac (Genesis 24:4), Jacob (Genesis 28:2) and Samson (Judges 14:3). However, this requirement was broadened later to include anyone within the nation of Israel. The Israelites were expressly

forbidden to marry foreigners in case this should lead to spiritual apostasy (Exodus 34:15, 16; Deuteronomy 7:3, 4). Even in the postexilic period we see Nehemiah berating the Jews who had returned to Judah for intermarrying with foreigners (Nehemiah 13:23-28).

Along with these laws about marriage to foreigners were the rules about marriage within the family. For example, a man was prohibited from marrying his aunt (Numbers 26:59). Incest between a man and his daughter, or between a woman and her son, or between brother and sister was strictly forbidden (Leviticus 18:7-9). In-laws were also forbidden to marry (Leviticus 18:8-17). A man must not be married to two sisters at the same time (Leviticus 18:18). The reasons behind these laws were wise both from a physical and a spiritual viewpoint. Their intent was to maintain purity in Israel.

DIVORCE

The Old Testament, while accepting the right to divorce, added careful legislation to protect women from being unfairly treated. However lax the Old Testament law may appear in the light of New Testament teaching, it was far superior to what was condoned outside Israel.

The particular Old Testament passage dealing with divorce to which our Lord referred in Matthew 19, in talking with the Pharisees, is Deuteronomy 24:1-4. In this passage we read: "If a man marries a woman who becomes displeasing to him because he finds something indecent about her, and he writes her a certificate of divorce, gives it to her and sends her from his house, and if after she leaves his house she becomes the wife of another man, and her second husband dislikes her and writes her a certificate of divorce, gives it to her and sends her from his house, or if he dies, then her first husband, who divorced her, is not allowed to marry her again after she has been defiled. That would be detestable in the eyes of the Lord. Do not bring sin upon the land the Lord your God is giving you as an inheritance."

The crucial words in this context are "he finds something indecent about her." Just what is meant by this phrase has been the subject of much discussion. However, in the light of Jewish rabbinical teaching it would appear that the reference was to some kind of marital unchastity. Whatever it was, the writing of the bill of divorcement was not so much to give permission as to set a limit. Its intent was the protection of the divorcée as well as the preservation of the institution of marriage. A woman, if divorced by her husband, could not without reason be put out on the street but had to be given the proper protection and provision of a legal divorce document.

Clearly the law permitting divorce allowed remarriage, but with the proviso that once a man had divorced his wife he was not allowed to remarry her. The Lord explained that Moses' law was given because of the hardness of man's sinful heart. Although divorce was undesirable and against God's order in creation, Moses knew that it might be better to sever a marriage relationship than persist in something which had already been defiled and broken through sin. Once again we are reminded that only as man accepts God's will for his own life can he live in harmony with other men and women.

STUDY QUESTIONS

1. Consider the relative merits and problems of "arranged marriages."

2. In what ways is Rebekah's preparation for marriage exemplary (Genesis 24)?

3. What lessons may we learn from Rebekah's treatment of her two sons?

4. How practical is the Old Testament law for newlyweds today?

5. Idolatry was considered "fornication" in the Old Testament. Are there spiritual parallels for Christians today?

6. Consider the importance of what the Bible teaches about monogamy.

7. What would you do if, as a missionary, you served in a culture that accepted polygamy?

C H A P T E R T H R E E

FAMILY IN
THE OLD TESTAMENT

The writers of the Old Testament laid great stress on the importance of family life. They saw the family not only as the building block of humanity but as the training ground for life and responsibility within society. For them, in a very real sense, Israel was "one family under God."

Israel's social life sprang from her common tribal and family roots. For example, when Israel's prophets referred to "the Fathers," their hearers could identify whom they meant immediately. They knew who they were and prided themselves on being the descendants of Abraham, Isaac, Jacob, and the twelve patriarchs. Even in the New Testament, when Paul listed the advantages belonging to Israel he wrote, "Theirs are the patriarchs, and from them is traced the human ancestry of Christ" (Romans 9:5).

Each Jewish family saw itself as a representation or visible miniature of one of those patriarchal families. They were aware of their tribal background and parents named their children after famous members of their own tribe. Saul of Tarsus was no doubt named for his famous Benjamite ancestor, King Saul.

It is here that we see the significance of the rite of circumcision so carefully practiced by the Jews. Circumcision was not simply a ritual, but a covenant mark, a recognition of God's part in the birth and the keeping of their national family. Israel saw itself as a tightly knit nation committed to its belief in one God, Jehovah, and its covenant with him.

THE BLESSING OF CHILDREN

In Israel children were said to be God's gift to the family and they were to be protected and nurtured in the faith. The Psalmist's famous words express it well: "Sons are a heritage from the Lord, children a reward from him. Like arrows in the hands of a warrior are sons born in one's youth. Blessed is the man whose quiver is full of them. They will not be put to shame when they contend with their enemies in the gate" (Psalm 127:3-5).

Eve's response to the birth of Cain was, "With the help of the Lord I have brought forth a man" (Genesis 4:1). God's promise to Abraham and Sarah was, "I will bless her and will surely give you a son by her. I will bless her so that she will be a mother of nations; kings of peoples will come from her" (Genesis 17:16).

Leah's consolation in the face of her husband Jacob's favoritism toward her younger sister Rachel was, "It is because the Lord has seen my misery. Surely my husband will love me now. . . . Because the Lord heard that I am not loved, he gave me this one too. . . . Now at last my husband will become attached to me, because I have borne him three sons." (Genesis 29:32-34).

Jacob, exasperated by Rachel's complaint about her barrenness, became angry and asked her, "Am I in the place of God, who has kept you from having children?" (Genesis 30:2).

Once delivered from her affliction, Rachel rejoiced: "God has vindicated me; he has listened to my plea, and given me a son" (Genesis 30:6).

Later in the story, when Esau saw Jacob's family approaching, he asked, "Who are these with you?" Jacob replied, "They are the children God has graciously given your servant" (Genesis 33:5). Finally, in the beautiful story of Ruth, we read about the Bethlehem elders giving their blessing to Boaz and Ruth: "May the Lord make the woman who is coming into your home like Rachel and Leah, who together built up the house of Israel. May you have standing in Ephrathah and be famous in Bethlehem. Through the offspring the Lord gives you by this young woman, may your family be like that of Perez, whom Tamar bore to Judah (Ruth 4:11, 12).

This idea of children being a special mark of divine favor is further confirmed by what the Bible says about barrenness or sterility. Not to have children was regarded as a mark of disgrace, if not of divine displeasure, as the following Scriptures indicate: "Then God remembered Rachel; he listened to her and opened her womb. She became pregnant and gave birth to a son and said, 'God has taken away my disgrace' " (Genesis 30:22, 23).

"But to Hannah he gave a double portion because he loved her, and the Lord had closed her womb. . . . And she made a vow, saying, 'O Lord Almighty, if you will only look upon your servant's misery and remember me, and not forget your servant but give her a son, then I will give him to the Lord for all the days of his life' " (1 Samuel 1:5, 11).

Similarly when barrenness was healed there was great rejoicing: "He settles the barren woman in her home as a happy mother of children. Praise the Lord" (Psalm 113:9); and " 'Sing, O barren woman, you who never bore a child; burst into song, shout for joy, you who were never in labor; because more are the children of the desolate woman than of her who has a husband,' says the Lord" (Isaiah 54:1).

This may all sound very strange to our contraceptive pill-popping, abortion-on-demand society, but it is a very typical element of the Old Testament view of family.

Childbirth was a very special event and a time of community rejoicing in Israel. It involved, as well, some special ritual requirements for the parents and especially the mother (Leviticus 12:3-8; Ruth 4:13-17; Luke 2:21-24). The postnatal cleansing rites appear to have varied with the gender of the offspring. Whatever the spiritual meaning of these events, they were probably of hygienic value as well. The dedication, presentation, and redemption of offspring were also ways of expressing gratitude to God and a sense of dependence on him.

MOTHERHOOD
Along with its blessing on childbirth and family life, the Old Testament idealizes motherhood. This has special meaning in light of the role of the male in Hebrew society. Indeed, whether with purpose or not, the Old Testament writers appear to present stories of weak fathers and strong mothers. The father may

have had influence, but it was usually the mother who offered moral fiber and spiritual integrity to her children.

We read for example of the courage and ingenuity of Jochebed, servant of Jehovah and mother of Moses (Exodus 2); of the common sense of Manoah's wife, Samson's mother (Judges 13:23); and of the prayers of Hannah, the mother of Samuel (1 Samuel 1). These are just a sampling of the "mothers in Israel" (Judges 5:7) who, like Rachel and Leah, helped build up the nation (Ruth 4:11).

In reading the Old Testament one can see the truth of the adage: "Behind every good man there is a good mother." In fact, we may go further and observe that, when compared with fathers like Noah, Lot, Eli, Samuel, David, Solomon, or half a dozen others, the Bible mothers take the honors. It is true that a Jew is a Jew not because his father is Jewish but because his mother is.

THE PATERNAL BLESSING

Another feature of Old Testament family life is the father's blessing on his offspring. This is clear in the patriarchal stories. For example, we have Noah's blessing on Shem and Japheth: "Blessed be the Lord, the God of Shem! May Canaan be the slave of Shem. May God extend the territory of Japheth; may Japheth live in the tents of Shem, and may Canaan be his slave" (Genesis 9:26, 27).

There is the rather sad tale of Isaac's blessing of Jacob and Esau told in Genesis 27. Whatever we may feel about Rebekah and Jacob's deceit, the story at least points out the serious light in which the paternal blessing was seen (Hebrews 12:17).

It is as though this blessing (given by the head of the family or clan) was an attempt to reach into the future to influence the coming generations. This is very clear in the rather strange story of Jacob's blessing of his grandsons, the sons of Joseph. We see Jacob quite deliberately switching his hands so that his right hand rests on the head of Ephraim, the younger son, and his left hand on Manasseh (Genesis 48:15-22). Perhaps the most famous is Jacob's blessing on his twelve sons as they assemble at his deathbed (Genesis 49).

THE FIRSTBORN

A further important feature of family life in the Old Testament is the privilege and blessing given to the firstborn. Many reasons have been given for this custom. The clearest one is that since childbirth was regarded as a token of divine blessing, the first child "to open the womb" signaled God's approval on the whole family. For example, when Jacob blessed Reuben he said, "Reuben, you are my firstborn, my might, the first sign of my strength, excelling in honor, excelling in power" (Genesis 49:3).

The most famous Old Testament story about the firstborn is that of Esau's selling of his birthright to Jacob for a bowl of lentil soup. Although we may condemn Jacob's scheming, the Bible condemned Esau, who "despised his birthright" (Genesis 25:34). It is clear that firstborn rights involved more than the father's wealth.

There are indications that the firstborn honor might be given to any member of the family, quite apart from order of birth. This is the way some commentators interpret the story of Joseph. We read:

"Now Israel loved Joseph more than any of his other sons, because he had been born to him in his old age; and he made a richly ornamented robe for him. When his brothers saw that their father loved him more than any of them, they hated him and could not speak a kind word to him" (Genesis 37:3, 4).

Joseph's beautiful coat may have been "a coat of long sleeves" (which is a possible translation of the Hebrew). Such coats were evidently given to firstborn sons, as a sort of token of their position. This would seem to account for his brothers' anger. It seems unlikely that mere favoritism of the kind hinted in this story would have caused Jacob's brothers to mistreat him as they did (Genesis 37).

Then there are the words spoken first of David, but ultimately of Christ: "I will also appoint him my firstborn, the most exalted of the kings of the earth. I will maintain my love to him forever, and my covenant with him will never fail. I will establish his line forever, his throne as long as the heavens endure" (Psalm 89:27-29).

From this reference it is clear that "firstborn" may be used as a title of honor and dignity, having no regard for who is older. This helps us understand such New Testament references as Colossians 1:15 and 18. In this greatest of all passages about Christ we read, "He is the image of the invisible God, the firstborn of all creation. . . . and he is the head of the body, the church; he is the beginning and the firstborn from among the dead, so that in everything he might have the supremacy."

Some who deny the deity of the Lord Jesus use these words of Paul's to support the idea that Christ is the firstborn in the sense of "first chronologically, of all God's creatures." However, quite apart from the context, which clearly denies such an idea, we now see that Paul was using "firstborn" in a true biblical sense. His point was that Christ is the absolute supreme, sovereign Lord of all, by the good pleasure of the Father.

Before we leave this subject we should see how significant the Old Testament concept of firstborn is, because of the story of Israel's great deliverance from Egypt. In that story the nation of Israel is regarded as Jehovah's firstborn son and Pharaoh is warned that if he does not release Israel, that judgment will be meted out on his firstborn son (Exodus 4:22).

As the story unfolds we see Pharaoh's refusal leading to the final plague, the slaying of every firstborn male of man and beast (Exodus 11). The deliverance of the Hebrew firstborn sons by the shed blood of the Passover lamb is to be remembered both in the Passover feast and in the dedication of the firstborn sons to God. Firstborn animals were to be sacrificed, but the sons were to be redeemed (Exodus 13:12, 13). The law showed that the tribe of Levi was to take the place of the firstborn. A money payment was made in lieu of the difference in number of the firstborn over the Levites (Numbers 3:40-51). This ransom payment was made to dedicate a firstborn son. Of course, this is the background of the beautiful story told in Luke 2:22-24. We cannot go into this here but it is in this ritual that the great Christian doctrine of redemption is pictured.

STUDY QUESTIONS
1. Why is "family" so important in the Old Testament?

2. Should economics govern the size of a family?
3. In what ways can children be a blessing?
4. What wrong attitudes may lead to child abuse?
5. Consider the virtues and responsibilities of motherhood.
6. Should rights of the firstborn be considered important today?
7. What are the dangers of showing favoritism in a family?
8. What do you consider a father's special responsibilities?

RESPECT FOR FAMILY AND HERITAGE

INSTRUCTION OF CHILDREN

The Old Testament put great stress on the parents' need to instruct their children in spiritual matters. For example, when the great *Shema*, that most fundamental statement of Jewish belief, was pronounced, it was immediately followed by the command that it be taught to the children: "Hear, O Israel: The Lord our God, the Lord is one. Love the Lord your God with all your heart and with all your soul and with all your strength. These commandments that I give you today are to be upon your hearts. Impress them on your children. Talk about them when you sit at home and when you walk along the road, when you lie down and when you get up" (Deuteronomy 6:4-7).

This passage suggests several things. First, parents must make sure their children understand the nature of God. Second, children must be well instructed in the great principles of the law. Third, this training must be given along with consistent parental example (Deuteronomy 11:18-21). The teaching of children started at an early age and was quite systematic. We read: "Who is it he is trying to teach? To whom is he explaining the message? To children weaned from their milk, to those just taken from the breast?"

For it is: "Do and do, do and do, rule on rule, rule on rule. A little here, a little there."

Another part of the teaching children received was about the great days of Israel's history. This was done at the great national feasts such as Passover. We read, for example, "When you enter the land that the Lord will give you as he promised, observe this ceremony. And when your children ask you, 'What does this ceremony mean to you?' then tell them, 'It is the Passover sacrifice to the Lord, who passed over the houses of the Israelites in Egypt and spared our houses when he struck down the Egyptians' " (Exodus 12:25-27).

In another place Moses said, "On that day tell your son, 'I do this because of what the Lord did for me when I came out of Egypt' " (Exodus 13:8).

The words of Psalm 78 suggest that the study of history not only made children aware of God's providence but also gave them a sense of nationhood and of having a part in God's acts. It would also have the good effect of keeping the children from making the same mistakes as their forebears. The Psalmist wrote, "I will open my mouth in parables, I will utter things hidden from of old—things we have heard and known, things our fathers have told us. We will not hide them from their children; we will tell the next generation the praiseworthy deeds of the Lord, his power, and the wonders he has done" (Psalm 78:2-4).

It is in the light of such careful and consistent

instruction that the writer of Proverbs can promise: "Train a child in the way he should go, and when he is old he will not turn from it" (Proverbs 22:6).

RESPECT AND CONCERN FOR PARENTS

If the Old Testament is clear in its instruction to parents, so is it in its advice to children to respect their parents. Indeed, at the very heart of the Ten Commandments we find these words: "Honor your father and your mother, so that you may live long in the land your God is giving you" (Exodus 20:12).

Many scholars divide the Ten Commandments into two groups, commandments one through five, duties godward; and six through ten, duties manward. If this analysis is correct, and our Lord's summation of them appears to confirm that it is (Mark 12:30, 31), then duty toward parents is a part of that section of the law that represents our duties to God. In one sense, as far as their children are concerned, parents are visible stand-ins for God. Filial respect is akin to worship, and not properly divorced from it. Both Jesus and Paul cite the fifth commandment in support of their own teaching (Matthew 15:4; Ephesians 6:1).

Many other Old Testament passages teach this idea of respect and concern for parents. For example: "The fear of the Lord is the beginning of knowledge, but fools despise wisdom and discipline. Listen, my son, to your father's instruction and do not forsake your mother's teaching. They will be a garland to grace your head and a chain to adorn your neck" (Proverbs 1:7-9).

"My son, keep your father's commands and do not forsake your mother's teaching. Bind them upon your heart forever; fasten them around your neck. When you walk, they will guide you; when you sleep, they will watch over you; when you awake, they will speak to you" (Proverbs 6:20-22).

"Listen to your father, who gave you life, and do not despise your mother when she is old" (Proverbs 23:22).

This mutual respect of parents and children accounts very largely for the stability and strength of Bible families. Some of these families were anything but exemplary, but on the whole they can certainly teach us "moderns" much. In fact, even today orthodox Jewish families don't have the alienation and breakups so common in western society. Of course, it might be argued that this is as much the result of the emphasis on personal morality as on family tradition.

CORRECTION AND PUNISHMENT OF CHILDREN
The Old Testament stresses not only the need to instruct children but also to require them to obey. Where such teaching is refused, or where there is disobedience, then there must be discipline and correction. This correction may take the form of corporal punishment. We may well give careful heed to these passages from Proverbs: "He who spares the rod hates his son, but he who loves him is careful to discipline him" (Proverbs 13:24).

"Folly is bound up in the heart of a child, but the rod of discipline will drive it far from him" (Proverbs 22:15).

"Do not withhold discipline from a child; if you punish him with the rod, he will not die" (Proverbs 23:13).

"The rod of correction imparts wisdom, but a child left to itself disgraces his mother. . . . Discipline your son, and he will give you peace; he will bring delight to your soul" (Proverbs 29:15, 17).

Some very stern words are reserved for stubborn and rebellious children; for example, we read, "Anyone who attacks his father or mother must be put to death. . . . Anyone who curses his father or mother must be put to death" (Exodus 21:15, 17; Leviticus 20:9).

Then there is the other famous passage concerning the ritual sentence upon the "stubborn and rebellious son." Although we have no example of this sentence ever having been carried out, its presence in the law must have been a salutary deterrent. It reads: "If a man has a stubborn and rebellious son who does not obey his father and mother and will not listen to them when they discipline him, his father and mother shall take hold of him and bring him to the elders at the gate of the town. They shall say to the elders, 'This son of ours is stubborn and rebellious. He will not obey us. He is a profligate and a drunkard.' Then all the men of his town shall stone him to death. You must purge evil from among you. All Israel will hear of it and be afraid" (Deuteronomy 21:18).

FAMILY INHERITANCES

Family inheritances were important in Israel and were to be carefully preserved. According to the law, the land belonged to Jehovah and was distributed under a sort of perpetual lease to the various tribes and families. This was in keeping with the plans made in the time of Joshua. Each tribe was given an area for occupation. The details are set out in the book of Joshua, chapters 13-21. The only tribe not given a territorial inheritance was the tribe of Levi (Joshua 14:3). In fact they were allotted forty-eight cities and environs for their dwellings but their inheritance was said to be "the Lord." The Levites were to be provided for out of the offerings the other tribes made to Jehovah (Numbers 18:24). Since they were to be engaged full time in the service of the Lord, they were not expected to have to farm or trade to earn a living. It was always a sign of spiritual declension in Israel when the Levites had to "go back to the fields" (Nehemiah 13:10).

The family inheritance was regarded as a sacred trust or stewardship from the Lord and was held in perpetuity. Such family real estate was not traded in the same way that properties are bought and sold today. In the event that land was sold off to settle outstanding debts, it had to be returned to the original family owners in the Year of Jubilee. Further, when such real estate was being assessed, the price of it would be based on how close the sale date was to the next Year of Jubilee (Leviticus 25).

This attitude toward the family inheritance made people very aware of their "native heath." Families could easily identify their ancestral plot. It helped strengthen family ties and gave a person a sense of belonging in a community, which was, in effect, his extended family. Even the ancestral burial sites nearby would remind a person that he or she was part of the past as well as the present. This is perhaps the meaning of that rather quaint phrase in Scripture, "he slept with his fathers." There must have been some comfort in knowing that one was a part of the ongoing stream of a family.

Second, there were proper laws of succession and inheritance which would help prevent strife among children of a family (Numbers 27:1-11). These laws governed the allocation of family inheritances and were administered by the "lot and line" method. It is this technique David speaks of in the Psalm where he uses this figure of speech: "Lord you have assigned me my portion and my cup; you have made my lot secure. The boundary lines have fallen for me in pleasant places; surely I have a delightful inheritance" (Psalm 16:5, 6).

The community elders would prepare a rough map of land to be assigned. They would draw up plot lines with survey marks, then property would be distributed according to the casting of lots. This method not only made for fair allotment but also gave people a sense of God's overruling and direction in these quite mundane affairs of their lives. They could live gratefully and dependently on God and each other.

No doubt this sense of family inheritance and divine providence would be less pronounced in the urban sites than in the rural areas. But even in the towns, villages by our standards, the sense of family tradition was still fostered. In the nativity story we see Joseph and Mary returning "to Bethlehem the town of David, because he belonged to the house and line of David" (Luke 2:4). Rome's census-takers saw the value of bringing people back to their ancestral places.

Third, families with land would be much more settled and responsible and less likely to become nomadic. Even if, through marriage, famine, or other causes, a family moved away from the ancestral setting, they must have retained the knowledge and memory of home. We see this in the story of Naomi. It is clearly a great relief for her to be back in Bethlehem in Judah. Moab had provided temporary shelter and sustenance in time of famine, but there was really no place like home (Ruth 1:20, 21). This same lovely story gives us a further insight into the "lot and line" land allocation just mentioned. We read for example that when Ruth set out to glean in the fields of Bethlehem, "As it turned out, she found herself working in the field belonging to Boaz, who was from the clan of Elimelech" (Ruth 2:3). From this it seems that not only were large tracts recognized as allotted to certain families, but even sections of these fields.

The clearest lesson to be drawn from all these Scriptures is a view of what the family should be. Among God's chosen people, what one thought of his family, its relationships, its history, and its future were seen as a reflection of what one thought about God himself. This fact might help us understand why families today are in serious trouble.

STUDY QUESTIONS
1. How can we help children understand about God?
2. What part should the Bible play in the teaching of children?
3. In what ways can children be encouraged to respect older people?
4. Consider methods of disciplining children.
5. What are the advantages and disadvantages of raising children in a rural environment?
6. Consider the dangers of wealth in a family.
7. Suggest various ways of "conducting" family prayers.

PART TWO

JESUS' TEACHING ON MARRIAGE AND FAMILY LIFE

"And you, my child, will be called a prophet of the Most High; for you will go on before the Lord to prepare the way for him, to give his people the knowledge of salvation through the forgiveness of their sins, because of the tender mercy of our God, by which the rising sun will come to us from heaven to shine on those living in darkness and in the shadow of death, to guide our feet into the path of peace "

(Luke 1:76-79).

JESUS' TEACHING ABOUT MARRIAGE

"Haven't you read," he replied, "that at the beginning the Creator 'made them male and female,' and said, 'For this reason a man will leave his father and mother and be united to his wife, and the two will become one flesh'? So they are no longer two, but one. Therefore what God has joined together, let man not separate" (Matthew 19:4-6).

Our Lord not only set great store by marriage but he offers clear and direct precepts about it. His most complete discourse on the subject is found in this passage from Matthew's Gospel. Although this is brief, and given largely in the context of an answer to a test question posed by a group of Pharisees, it is fairly complete. It is immediately clear that Jesus is not teaching a new view of marriage but is restating and reinforcing the divine order in creation. By doing this he shows that marriage is a part of God's plan for man.

THE SEXES COMPLEMENT EACH OTHER

Jesus noted that, "at the beginning the Creator made them male and female." Although he did not quote the whole of Genesis 1:27, without doubt he had it all in view. God made man in his own image, male and female, two distinct yet complementary genders. Jesus was showing that human sexuality originated with God.

For Jesus, man is man and woman is woman, but neither is complete without the other. In other words, heterosexuality is fundamental to our Lord's view of marriage. For him the difference of the sexes is what makes them complementary, which is basic to their role in society as planned by God.

Jesus' teaching rejects the unisex philosophy of the liberationist as well as the perversion of the homosexual. For Jesus, maleness and femaleness do not suggest conflict, strife, and competitiveness, but harmony and wholeness. Maleness and femaleness are parts of what it means to be created in the image of God. From the two we learn something about the nature of God.

THE IMPORTANCE OF MONOGAMY

Our Lord's acceptance of the creation order is a clear statement concerning monogamy. He spoke of a relationship existing between *one* man and *one* woman. Notice he talked about "a man" and "his wife" and of "the *two*" becoming "*one* flesh." Then he added, "So they are no longer *two*, but *one*." There is not the slightest evidence that Jesus ever condoned polygamy. For him, as for the Scripture as a whole, God's plan is one man for one woman (John 4:16-18). Wherever we find polygamy practiced or tolerated in

Bible stories, we find spiritual declension and problems. Only by the wildest stretch of imagination or by "wresting the Scripture," would we suggest that the Bible tolerates bigamy or polygamy. The fact that it recognizes the existence of these aberrations, and regulates their excesses, says nothing about God's condoning either.

THE NEW FAMILY UNIT

In his further quotation, "For this cause shall a man leave his father and mother and shall cleave to his wife" (Genesis 2:27), Jesus is reemphasizing the importance of each new family unit. The King James Version makes a play on words and contrasts "leave" with "cleave." Jesus seems to infer that only if a man (viewed in this context as the initiator) recognizes the importance of "leaving" his natural family and of "cleaving" to his wife, can a marriage succeed. There can be no "cleaving" unless there be a "leaving." This does not mean that a man severs all connection with his parents and family, any more than that he will cease to appreciate his heritage. What it means is that he deliberately accepts the responsibility of sticking to his wife and supporting her as his spouse, resisting the wrong kind of pressure from the in-laws.

No marriage will work if either party to it thinks that the answer to any and every problem can be found in "running home to mother." Newly married couples are well advised to learn all they can from their own upbringing and to apply to their own relationship any valuable lessons learned. However, at the same time, because their parents did things in a certain way does not mean that that is the only way or even the best way. Christian marriage does carry what may sometimes appear to be awesome responsibilities; but it is good to remember that the Lord who offers this counsel on marriage is the same One who promises to be with us to carry whatever load we will entrust to him (Matthew 28:20; 1 Peter 5:4).

UNITY IN MARRIAGE

Our Lord insisted on the oneness of husband and wife in the marriage bond. This is clear both from his quotation from Genesis, ". . . and be united to his wife, and the two will become one flesh"; and from his own comment: "Therefore what God has joined together, let man not separate."

The Greek word *proskollēthēsetai* quoted here from the Septuagint version of Genesis 2:4 and translated "united" in the New International Version, comes from *kollaō* which means literally, "to glue" or "to cement." In Matthew the verb is in the passive voice and reflexive, thus further stressing the closeness of the bond. Obviously *kollaō* is used metaphorically here; but it is in the imagery of the word that we catch its true meaning. It suggests that just as two pieces of material, once glued together, cannot be separated without damage to both, so two people once joined in marriage cannot be separated without hurt to both. Hence the wisdom of Jesus' injunction, "let not man separate." His words have special meaning in this context, since not only is marriage being discussed, but also divorce. Jesus' point is that if we better understood the closeness of the "uniting," we would better understand the tragedy and hurt of the "separating."

There is no doubt that the unity mentioned here,

"the two shall be one flesh," while including physical union, means something much deeper than that. It also includes psychological bonding and, in the case of a Christian marriage, spiritual fulfillment. As a matter of fact, when a man and woman are united in marriage and live together in the fullness of that beautiful relationship, they seem to be fused into one. As it has been well expressed, "in the arithmetic of marriage, one plus one equals one." Such is the beautiful synthesizing of marriage, that often even the temperamental differences that may once have attracted two diverse people to each other, tend to disappear. Many couples, after living together for years, tend to become very much alike in outlook, desire, expression, vocabulary, activity, and sometimes even in appearance.

THE SANCTITY OF MARRIAGE

Jesus words, "what God has joined together, let man not separate" further suggest that marriage should be something arranged by God. Whatever else this may imply, it tells us that marriage as an institution is sacred, and also that a marriage should be seen as a contract that is inviolable.

Practically speaking, we must admit that while there are many marriages that appear to have been "made in heaven," there are others that appear to have had their origin elsewhere. It is surely reading too much into Jesus' words to suggest that every marriage is arranged by God. However, it remains true that the God who performed the first wedding is still concerned about the success of every other marriage. In this sense there is a special sanctity about every true marriage. Let every bride and groom who seek true fulfillment and happiness remember this. If they in turn want God's blessing on their union, then let them try to seek God's direction and blessing before getting married. A marriage which is "in the Lord," to use Paul's phrase (1 Corinthians 7:39), is unbeatable and those who have been party to such will certainly rejoice that they have been "joined together by God."

THE PERMANENCE OF MARRIAGE

There can be no question that although Jesus spoke to the question of divorce in Matthew 19:9, he affirmed the idea of marriage as a permanent bond. His emphasis on the union in marriage, as well as his repeating the command for husband and wife to cleave together, made this plain. His further words, "What therefore God has joined together, let not man put asunder" are unequivocal on this subject.

Matthew 22:30-33 must also be considered in connection with Jesus' teaching on marriage. In these verses Jesus was talking with a group of Sadducees. These men, who represent the rationalists of their day, didn't believe in resurrection. They came with a hypothetical question based on the ancient custom of levirate marriages. They asked Jesus what would happen if a woman had been married to seven brothers in turn. "Now then," they asked, "at the resurrection whose wife will she be of the seven, since all of them were married to her?"

Jesus, who obviously rejected both their scepticism and their frivolous view of marriage, replied: "You are in error because you do not know the Scriptures or the power of God. At the resurrection people will neither marry nor be given in marriage; they will be like the angels in heaven" (Matthew 22:29, 30).

In these and the rest of the words that make up the Lord's answer to the Sadducees, he pointed out several things. First, there is a resurrection. Second, while human beings marry, the angels evidently do not. Third, God is alive and is the God of living people. Finally, while marriages are normal here and now, such relationships will not be contracted hereafter. This seems to imply that while human sexuality is significant on earth, it will not necessarily be so in the eternal state.

STUDY QUESTIONS
1. In what ways does Jesus legitimize marriage?
2. Could a case for celibacy be built on the teaching of Jesus? (See Matthew 19:4-11.)
3. How can we balance the two ideas of "cleaving" and "leaving"?
4. What things make for unity in marriage?
5. Why is marriage sacred?
6. Are there any biblical alternatives to permanence in marriage?
7. What lessons do we learn from Jesus' first miracle, at the wedding in Cana?

JESUS AND HIS EARTHLY FAMILY

Although the Lord said very little about family life, his other teachings and the example he set offer clear and dependable guidelines for happy family life.

The central event of Scripture is the miracle of the incarnation. Here, in time and space, is "God manifest in flesh" (1 Timothy 3:16). Aside from the theological meaning of the incarnation, this is the story of God who came to live in the context of an earthly family. We often call it the nativity story, but it is much more than that. It begins with the birth of Jesus but it goes on to show us how he, truly God and truly man, took his place very naturally, in a home. We should try to discover what some of the important lessons about home and family are, that we may learn and apply them to our situation today.

THE VALUE OF FAMILY HERITAGE

The geneaological tables presented by Matthew and

Luke are not just literary "fillers" or fictitious attempts to "humanize" a supernatural person. They are an accurate history of Jesus' earthly forebears. These written records remind us that Christianity is grounded in history, not mythology. Matthew and Luke tell us that Jesus had ordinary human ancestors and was part of a family tree, which was very important in Jewish society, where great store was placed on tribal association, ethnic purity, and family inheritances.

It appears that Matthew presented what we might call Jesus' legal descent through Joseph, while Luke described his physical descent through Mary. In Luke, Joseph, who is probably the son-in-law of Heli, is named instead of Mary.

We also believe in the miraculous virgin birth of Jesus. We understand that Jesus' humanity was "conceived of the Holy Ghost" (Matthew 1:20), and developed in the womb of the virgin Mary. Thus he could properly be described as the son of Mary and the Son of God. Obviously we are touching on profound, but yet reasonable mysteries, particularly in the light of our Lord's immaculate life.

Several facts emerge from even a cursory study of these genealogies. For example, we discover that Jesus was born of the Hebrew race. Matthew traced his family tree back to Abraham. Taking a wider view, Luke told us that the story of Jesus' humanity goes back to Adam. That is to say, he is a member of the whole human family. Further, we see that he was of royal descent.

Another important fact we learn from Matthew's genealogical table is that while Jesus was tied in to a human posterity, he was not limited by his heredity. From a Jewish point of view, it was unusual that four women apart from Mary were mentioned in Jesus' family tree and that each of them is of questionable character for one reason or another. This fact should encourage us, showing that we are not inescapably determined by our heredity, whether for good or ill. We may be grateful for our family heritage, but we must also remember that whatever else we inherit with our genes, we do not inherit God's salvation and the privilege of being a part of God's family. That blessing depends on our personal response to the grace of God offered through the person and saving work of Christ.

In considering the Lord's earthly, family heritage we are reminded of the great value of the extended family. It must have been a very difficult time for Mary as she awaited the birth of the baby Jesus. Whatever she knew about the baby's supernatural conception would have sounded strange to her acquaintances. Living as she did in a closely knit village community, it would have been impossible for Mary to escape the questions and gossip of her friends and neighbors.

Perhaps it was with this in mind that Mary's mother, traditionally known as Anne, decided to send her daughter off to Ein Kerem, a little village nestling in the Judean hills, just a few miles from Jerusalem. It was there that their relative Elizabeth, wife of Zacharias, lived. She herself was already six months pregnant, despite her advanced years. In fact it may have been this miracle that was happening to Elizabeth that had encouraged Mary's mother to accept her daughter's unusual explanation of her own condition. We can only conjecture (Luke 1:39-45).

In any case, Mary's going to Zacharias' home

served several purposes. It meant for example, on the one hand, that Elizabeth had the benefit of Mary's help in the final three months of her own confinement as she awaited the birth of her son, John. Elizabeth's husband, Zacharias, was old himself and unable to be of much practical assistance because of his temporary inability to speak. Under these circumstances, Mary's presence would have been most helpful. Then, on the other hand, Zacharias' home provided a haven for Mary. While she was there, Elizabeth would have been a great encouragement to Mary, and able to cheer her up during her pregnancy.

The miracle that took place, as Mary arrived at Elizabeth's home and greeted her, would have been a further confirmation to Mary of what she already knew. It would certainly have shown Elizabeth and Anne, who may well have traveled from Nazareth with her daughter, that Mary was the object of God's special blessing. The whole story gives one the feeling of the comfort that was mutually available to the members of Jesus' extended family and reminds us of the blessing it can be today.

We might take note of one other event in this connection. It took place as Jesus was hanging on the cross. Despite his own suffering he was concerned for his mother Mary and very tenderly committed her into the care of his disciple, John. Mary's sister, some think, was Salome, the mother of John and James, Zebedee's sons (John 19:25; Mark 15:40; Matthew 27:56). If we are right in our understanding of their relationship, then at the end of his earthly life as at its beginning, Jesus recognized the helpfulness of the extended family.

THE SIGNIFICANCE AND WORTH OF
ANTENATAL LIFE

The story of Mary's visit to Elizabeth's home can also help us in regard to the current discussion about abortions and our attitude toward unborn children. This is how Luke, himself a physician, describes what happened, "When Elizabeth heard Mary's greeting, the baby leaped in her womb and Elizabeth was filled with the Holy Spirit. In a loud voice she exclaimed, 'Blessed are you among women, and blessed is the child you will bear! But why am I so favored, that the mother of my Lord should come to me? As soon as the sound of your greeting reached my ears, the baby in my womb leaped for joy. Blessed is she who has believed that what the Lord has said to her will be accomplished!' " (Luke 1:41-45).

Whether we wish to explain this event in physiological, psychological, or spiritual terms, one thing is evident. Luke described what was in Elizabeth's womb as a "baby" and not merely a "fetus." For him, here was a human being, capable of sensation and intelligent response. No doubt we are intended to understand that Elizabeth was given special supernatural insight, and the significant movement of the child in her womb confirmed this revelation to her.

Elizabeth's greeting of Mary as "mother of my Lord" confirms also that although Mary was in the very initial stage of her own pregnancy, she too was carrying a real human child. One wonders if anyone today has ever thought what might have happened if either Mary or Elizabeth had opted for abortions. Either of them might have argued, at least in the idiom of current abortion-on-demand proponents, that they had "grounds for therapeutic abortion." Their social and religious conditioning helped them to think in much more wholesome terms. They were filled with thanksgiving and praise to God for his goodness. Any doubt we may have about this will be quickly dispelled if we read Mary's beautiful words (Luke 1:46-55).

THE NORMALCY OF CHILDBIRTH AND FAMILY LIFE

Many well-meaning people, even some Christians among them, entertain the idea that marriage and procreation are God's second best. Even the Christian church has, on some occasions in the past, tended to glorify celibacy and question the propriety of marriage and healthy sexual relationships. Even such men as Tertullian and Augustine spoke of marriage as if it were legalized adultery.

The story of the birth of Jesus certainly speaks to these attitudes. Granted, Jesus was born of a virgin and not as a result of the normal conception process. Nevertheless, he was physically born from the womb of Mary who subsequently, in accordance with Jewish custom and procedure, went through the usual purification ceremony associated with child birth (Luke 2:22). Furthermore, we see that, according to the Bible, after Jesus' birth, Mary and her husband Joseph became the parents of several children (Matthew 1:25; Mark 6:3; John 7:5).

In other words, the nativity story encourages us to recognize that marriage, procreation, and responsible family life are perfectly normal and a part of God's plan for man.

THE IMPORTANCE OF PARENTAL PIETY

We know very little about the private lives of Mary and Joseph. However, from what we are told about them in Scripture, we know that they were exemplary in piety. They evidently ordered their lives in accordance with the directions and requirements of the Word of God (Luke 2:22-24, 27, 39, 42), especially in the matter of Jesus' childhood. It was no accident that Jesus was born and raised in the family and home of people like Joseph and Mary.

Consider first what Luke tells about Mary. Although she was probably only a teenager at the time of Jesus' birth, Mary was obviously a very special and spiritually mature girl. In keeping with the custom of that day, she had been promised and betrothed to Joseph. This contract might well have been made when Mary was quite young and would normally be confirmed by both parties when they were of responsible age. The emphasis placed on the betrothal of Joseph and Mary in the Nativity story suggests that they both agreed to the betrothal and in due course would be united in marriage. Once this stage of commitment had been reached the relationship could only be severed by a proper divorce (Matthew 1:19).

Luke spoke of Mary's purity. She was still a virgin (*parthenos*) when she received Gabriel's announcement. This does not mean simply that she was a young woman of marriageable age. For that Luke would have used another Greek word, *neanis*. Whatever her relationship to Joseph, this word implies that she had not had sexual relations with any man.

Second, Gabriel's words to Mary tell us that she

was the recipient of God's grace. It is unfortunate that the Greek word, *kecharitōmenē* , is mistranslated by the well-known Latin phrase *gratia plena,* which in turn becomes in English, "full of grace." Gabriel was not saying that Mary is a source of grace but that she is a recipient of grace. As someone has said, "Mary was not a mother of grace but a daughter of grace!" Whatever else Gabriel's words mean, they tell us that Mary's heart was open to receive the Lord's blessing. Not only was she a girl of great faith, who took God at his word (Luke 1:45), but she was totally available to be the instrument of the Holy Spirit (Luke 1:35; Matthew 1:20). The Bible nowhere suggests that she was other than someone who needed to be saved, like any other man or woman.

By comparison with Mary, Joseph tends to receive brief notice in most descriptions. However, he must have been a man of unusual faith who accepted God's word under the most difficult of circumstances (Matthew 1:20-25). Imagine how he must have felt upon discovering that Mary was pregnant. Despite this heart-rendering situation, Joseph's kindly spirit overcame any feeling of hatred or vindictiveness. Still unaware of the facts, at least as later explained to him by the angel of the Lord, Joseph decided that instead of subjecting Mary to public disgrace, he would quietly divorce her. It need not seem strange that he planned to divorce Mary although he was not married to her. As already noted, a betrothal in Jewish law was as much a commitment as marriage itself, and could only be dissolved by death or divorce.

Joseph, having now married Mary and become by that act the legal father of her expected child, named the baby Jesus (v. 25). He did so in obedience to the angel's command (v. 21) and as a public declaration of his intention to be known as the child's legal parent and guardian. When the angel addressed Joseph he called him, "Joseph, son of David," and in Matthew's official genealogy, we see Jesus' ancestry traced back through Joseph to David.

The faith and kindness of Joseph are everywhere evident in the nativity story and in the unfolding story of our Lord's life. For example, although he married Mary and took her to his home, prior to the actual birth of Jesus, he carefully and patiently refrained from physical union with her until after her baby was born. Then when the baby Jesus' life was threatened by the cruel scheme of Herod the Great (Matthew 2:6), it was Joseph who, in obedience to another divine revelation, courageously took Mary and her baby by night to safety in Egypt.

Upon the death of Herod, Joseph returned with Mary and Jesus, to a remote area of Nazareth in Galilee. There, in that unlikely place, Joseph followed his trade as a carpenter and provided for his family. As Jesus grew into boyhood and young manhood it would appear from the question asked in Mark 6:3, "Is not this the carpenter, the son of Mary?" that he had served his apprenticeship under Joseph. Perhaps Joseph died while Jesus was young, but it was not before he had spent long hours with his "son" at the carpenter's bench. As a responsible parent, Joseph had trained Jesus in the skills of his art.

Having considered the faith of Mary and Joseph, we must now look at them as husband and wife together and see how they accepted the responsibility of parenthood. The first thing we notice is their submission to Scripture. For example, on the eighth day of Jesus' life Joseph and Mary took him, presumably to Jerusalem, to have him circumcised in accordance with the law of Moses (Leviticus 12:3). Then about a month later, thirty-three days, according to the law (Leviticus 12:4), they were back at the temple again, this time "to present him to the Lord" and to comply with the law's requirements for the consecration of the firstborn (Luke 2:22-24; cf. Exodus 13:2-12). Their offering on this occasion indicated that they were poor people (Leviticus 12:8). It must have been a wonderful occasion for both of them as they listened to the prophetic utterances spoken about Jesus by the aged Simeon and Anna.

Another evidence of their being good parents is their appreciation of what we might call today "family church life." Luke tells us, for example, how Joseph and Mary joined in the annual Passover pilgrimage to Jerusalem. Since they lived in Nazareth, coming to Jerusalem meant a considerable expenditure of time and effort. We are not told specifically that they took Jesus with them on these occasions, but almost certainly they did. We do know that when he was twelve years old he went with them to Jerusalem, for his "bar mitzvah," no doubt. This was the occasion when Jesus remained in the temple to discuss the law with the teachers. Evidently Joseph and Mary's parental vigilance lapsed on this occasion and it took them three days to find Jesus. When they did find him they learned further lessons about his divine origin and mission.

The story of Jesus' special visit to the synagogue in Nazareth, following his baptism and temptation, throws some light on his home life. We read, "He went to Nazareth where he had been brought up, and the Sabbath day he went into the synagogue, as was his custom. And he stood up to read" (Luke 4:16).

Evidently Joseph and Mary had not only taken care of Jesus physically, but spiritually as well. They had, despite their poverty, made sure that their son was versed in the Scriptures. Of course, not only did Jesus learn from Mary and Joseph, but they were able to learn much from him. It is important for parents not only to teach and direct their children in the ways of the Lord but to be willing to learn from them as well. Such are the blessings of a godly home.

THE NEED FOR FILIAL RESPONSIBILITY

We can learn many lessons about the family from Jesus' life in Nazareth. There are few more beautiful family cameos than the one painted in Luke 2:51: "Then he went down to Nazareth with them and was obedient to them. But his mother treasured all these things in her heart. And Jesus grew in wisdom and stature, and in favor with God and man."

In this snapshot from the teenage years of Jesus we see an exemplary pattern for all young people. We see that Jesus was content even growing up in Nazareth, of all places. He submitted to his parents' wishes. As he grew in body so he grew in mind and spirit.

Jesus also took his full share of responsibility around the home. Here was one teenager who learned the disciplines of hard work. It is possible that Joseph died early. At least he disappears completely from the pages of Scripture. This would mean that Jesus became his mother's supporter and the breadwinner in the family while still quite young. From what we read about his family, we learn that they were not the most congenial or cooperative types (John 7:5; Matthew 13:57; Mark 3:21), at least in their earlier years. We also remember that the care Jesus had shown for his mother during his life he still offered in death (John 19:27). Again, here is a lovely example of the concern children should have for their aged parents.

THE BLESSING OF MARRIAGE AND HOME
A beautiful passage in the book of Common Prayer reads,

> Holy matrimony. . . . which holy estate Christ adorned and beautified with his presence, and first miracle that he wrought in Cana of Galilee (The form of Solemnization of Matrimony).

From this story of Jesus' first miracle (John 2) we can learn many lessons about our family life. First, we see that our Lord recognized the importance of the marriage celebration. Today, in all kinds of circles, we hear people in favor of "common law" living or "living together," and the idea of a formal marriage as passé. In the light of this it is good to remember that Jesus put his blessing on marriage not only by his presence but by doing his first miracle at one. A wedding service enables us to show that we believe in commitment, covenant, faithfulness, and legality. Our Lord's presence at Cana, like his precepts, approved these things.

His famous miracle at this wedding reminds us that, among other things, Jesus approves of our being happy. Not only is he willing to meet human emergencies but also to show his power on behalf of ordinary people. It is so easy to think of Jesus in terms of religion and church. It is much more important to see that he is with us in our homes and concerned about the everyday problems that we face in our family circles.

Our Lord's appreciation of home life and the understanding of human relationships can also be seen in some of his miracles. For example, he restored Peter's wife's mother (Matthew 8:14). He gave back a daughter to her bereaved parents (Luke 8:40-56). He cast out a demon and healed the daughter of the Syrophoenician woman (Mark 7:26-30). He healed a demoniac boy and an official's son, restoring them to their respective fathers (Mark 9:17-27; John 4:46-54). He raised a widow's son and gave him back to her (Luke 7:11-17); and finally, he raised his friend Lazarus from the grave and restored him to his home and sisters in Bethany (John 11:11-44).

Although he had no home of his own in adult life (Luke 9:58), Jesus was always happy to enjoy the warmth and hospitality of other people's homes. For example, we see him enjoying a visit to Peter's home at Capernaum (Matthew 8:14). He dined in the home of his disciple, Matthew (Matthew 9:9, 10). He accepted the hospitality of Simon the Pharisee (Luke 7:36), and was welcomed as a guest in Zacchaeus' home in Jericho (Luke 19:17). The home of Mary, Martha, and Lazarus in Bethany seemed to be one of his very favorite places (John 11:1-5). After his resurrection, one of his early appearings was in the context of the home at Emmaus (Luke 24:28-31).

While Jesus approved of and appreciated married life, he also recognized and demonstrated the possibility of fulfillment and happiness in the single life. Our Lord was not celibate to prove that such a life was more virtuous. His single state evidently was part of the sacrifice he accepted because of his unique commitment to the will of God and to the work of our salvation. He would allow nothing, not even normal human relationships, to distract him from his task.

The example of Jesus' life is full of help for us today in our family and home relationships. Let us never forget that he left the glory of his Father's eternal home and came to share fully in the life of an ordinary earthly family. He did this that we might be part of God's forever family and share in his heavenly home.

It is all so well expressed in the children's hymn:

I love to think though I am young,
My Savior was a child;
That Jesus walked this earth along,
With feet all undefiled.

He kept His Father's word of truth
As I am taught to do
And while He walked the paths of youth,
He walked in wisdom too.

That He who wore the thorny crown,
And tasted death's despair,
Had a kind mother like my own
And knew her love and care.

(E. Paxton Hood)

STUDY QUESTIONS
1. What is the importance of the genealogical tables in the nativity story?
2. Consider the social problem of Mary's pregnancy.

3. Examine the story of Mary in the Gospels. What lessons do we learn from her?

4. List the various details about Joseph's life found in the Gospels.

5. Under what circumstances, if any, can abortion be justified?

6. What features of parental piety help children most?

7. What lessons can we learn for family living today from Jesus' family?

THEOLOGY
AND FAMILY

In the last chapter we considered the Lord's teaching about family through his example. Here we shall begin to listen to his precepts. We will see, of course, that the two, his life and his teaching, were consistent. There was no need for Jesus to say, as do so many teachers, "Don't do as I do, but do as I tell you." He called his followers not only to obey his precepts but to follow his example.

Some of the Lord's teaching had an indirect bearing on the subject of family. Some of his parables, in fact, are set in the context of family life, and some of the principles he taught regarding God and man, while having deep theological implications, also relate to our daily lives in the context of home and family.

THE FATHERHOOD OF GOD
One of the distinctives of our Christian faith is our belief that God is our Father. This truth is referred to in the Old Testament; but we have to wait for Jesus'

teaching in the Gospels to hear that God is the Father of those who believe, in a personal sense.

In Hebrew thought God is seen as the Father of Israel. For example, in the commissioning of Moses, God said to him, "Then say to Pharaoh, 'This is what the Lord says: Israel is my firstborn son, and I told you, "Let my son go, so he may worship me." ' " (Exodus 4:22).

There is a similar idea in Hosea's prophecy: "When Israel was a child, I loved him, and out of Egypt I called my son" (Hosea 11:1).

Then God sent the prophet Nathan to David with this promise concerning Solomon, the type of the "theocratic king." "I will be his father, and he will be my son" (2 Samuel 7:14).

Finally, in Malachi, God is viewed as the Father of all men in the sense of being our Creator: "Have we not all one Father? Did not one God create us?" (Malachi 2:10).

Encouraging though these words must have been to Israel, the teaching of Jesus regarding God's fatherhood takes us much further. He told us that while God was his own Father in a unique sense, he is also the Father of each one who trusts in him.

There is a difference of emphasis between the two Gospels that deal particularly with God's father-hood—Matthew and John. In John the stress is typically theological; and there, God is seen as the Father of Jesus (John 10:18, 29, 30). In Matthew the emphasis is practical and God is introduced as "Our Father." There is a sense in which our experience of father-child relationship gives a special dimension to our Lord's revelation of God as Father.

As our Father, God anticipates our needs. We read "Do not be like [pagans], for your Father knows what you need before you ask him" (Matthew 6:8).

In another place Jesus said, "So do not worry, saying, 'What shall we eat?' or 'What shall we wear?' for the pagans run after all these things, and your heavenly Father knows that you need them" (Matthew 6:32).

As our Father, God listens to us: "If you, then, though you are evil, know how to give good gifts to your children, how much more will your Father in heaven give good gifts to those who ask him!" (Matthew 7:11).

That most famous of all prayers opens with the words: "Our Father in heaven" (Matthew 6:9).

God, as Father, forgives us: "Forgive us our debts, as we also have forgiven our debtors" (Matthew 6:12).

Further on in the passage we read: "For if you forgive men when they sin against you, your heavenly Father will also forgive you."

As Father, God is personally and intimately concerned about us: "And even the very hairs of your head are all numbered. So don't be afraid; you are worth more than many sparrows" (Matthew 10:29).

God shares his secrets with us: "Jesus replied, 'Blessed are you, Simon son of Jonah, for this was not revealed to you by man, but by my Father in heaven' " (Matthew 16:17).

God desires our companionship and honor: "Yet a time is coming and has now come when the true worshipers will worship the Father in spirit and in truth, for they are the kind of worshipers the Father seeks" (John 4:23).

As Father, God offers us security: "My Father, who has given them to me, is greater than all; no one can snatch them out of my Father's hand. I and the Father are one" (John 10:29, 30).

God loves us: "I am not saying that I will ask the Father on your behalf. No, the Father himself loves you because you have loved me and believed that I came from God" (John 16:26).

God expects us to behave like his children: "In the same way, let your light shine before men, that they may see your good deeds and praise your Father in heaven" (Matthew 5:16).

He told us to "be perfect, therefore, as your heavenly Father is perfect" (Matthew 5:48; Matthew 6:15).

THE NEW BIRTH

Another of our Lord's important spiritual lessons, related to our idea of family, is "regeneration." We are familiar with Jesus' talk with Nicodemus (John 3). He explained that in the same way that we enter our earthly family by physical birth, so we become children of God by the new birth. By the power of the Holy Spirit we are regenerated, "born from above," as Jesus puts it. We have a new heredity. This new birth is effected by the Holy Spirit as we receive the imperishable seed of the Word of God in the obedience of faith (John 3:8; 1 Peter 1:21-23). Again there are some interesting contrasts. Physical birth is said to be of natural descent, of human decision, and of a husband's will. In regeneration a person is said to be "born of God" (John 1:12, 13).

DIVINE KINSHIP

All who are born of God are obviously in the family of God. This is why Jesus taught that those who do the will of God are not only brothers and sisters but his kin (Matthew 12:50). Again, this saying of Jesus grew directly out of his own experience of family life (Matthew 12:46-50; John 7:3-5). While he valued his earthly family, he showed that there may be even a deeper kinship than that, the family into which we have been "born again." Just as those related by ties of nature should be concerned for each other, so should all who are in God's family (Matthew 7:3-5; 18:15, 21, 22).

THE HEAVENLY BRIDEGROOM

There is one other mention of marriage in the teaching of Jesus, where he refers to himself as the heavenly bridegroom. John the Baptist's disciples came with a question about fasting: " 'How is it that we and the Pharisees fast, but your disciples do not fast?' Jesus answered, 'How can the guests of the bridegroom mourn while he is with them? The time will come when the bridegroom will be taken from them; then they will fast' " (Matthew 9:14, 15).

By using this particular illustration Jesus appeared to be suggesting that the marital relationship should be accompanied by joy. He certainly would not have used this metaphor had he disapproved of marriage or considered it of lesser value than celibacy.

PARABLES

Five of our Lord's parables are clearly based on the idea of marriage and family life. Two of the five have a marriage as their setting: the parable of the marriage of the King's Son (Matthew 22:1-13) and the parable of the Ten Virgins (Matthew 25:1-13). In the former there is a dual thrust. First there is the marriage feast, which is the context of the story; and second, there is the excuse offered by one of the guests for not attending, according to the parallel narrative in Luke 14:20. The guest excused himself on the basis that, "I just got married, so I can't come."

Two other parables relate particularly to family situations, especially the relationship between fathers and sons: the parable of the Two Sons (Matthew 21:28-32), which stresses the importance of deeds over words; and the parable of the Prodigal Son (Luke 15:11-32). The second is probably the best known of all Jesus' parables and is a valuable lesson on family relationships quite apart from its spiritual lessons. The parable points out the danger of favoritism, the problem of family quarrels, the hazards of parental indulgence, the difficulties created by inheritances—but above all, the strength of parental love.

One other parable probably refers to an ancient betrothal custom, the one we usually call the parable of the Lost Silver (Luke 15:8-10). It is suggested that the anxiety of the woman in this story was occasioned by her having lost one piece of her ten-piece silver engagement necklace. The breaking of this silver cord was evidently a symbol of one of two things, unfaithfulness or death (Ecclesiastes 11:6).

Whatever else these parables tell us about life, marriage, and family, they clearly demonstrate our Lord's interest in this subject and his approval of and blessing upon the home.

STUDY QUESTIONS

1. How do you understand the idea of the fatherhood of God?

2. What is the danger of teaching "the universal fatherhood of God"?

3. What is the meaning of "born again"?

4. When is it right and when is it wrong to "listen to" our relations?

5. How does the idea of Christ the heavenly Bridegroom help today?

6. Can we learn anything from the biblical idea of betrothal?

7. Consider Jesus' "wedding parables."

JESUS AND FAMILY RESPONSIBILITIES

Jesus was part of a society which set great store by family life. In this as in so many other ethical matters, the Jews stood alone in the ancient world. Not only did they teach parental responsibility but also the need for children to take care of their aged parents, ideas which form an essential part of the Old Testament record.

PARENTS' CONCERN FOR CHILDREN

The value of children. When Jesus was questioned by his disciples about greatness in the kingdom of heaven, he called a little child and had him stand among them. He said: "I tell you the truth, unless you change and become like little children, you will never enter the kingdom of heaven. Therefore, whoever humbles himself like this child is the greatest in the kingdom of heaven. And whoever welcomes a little child like this in my name welcomes me. But if anyone causes one of these little ones who believe in me to sin, it would be better for him to have a large millstone hung around his neck and to be drowned in the depths of the sea" (Matthew 18:2-6).

It is surprising that these strong words of Jesus, among the harshest he uttered, should be spoken about children. Obviously he set great store by them and placed an eternal worth upon them. He saw children as simple, uncomplicated, and trusting. A little later the Lord said, "See that you do not look down on one of these little ones. For I tell you that their angels in heaven always see the face of my Father in heaven" (Matthew 18:10).

Later he spoke again of children: "Let the little children come to me, and do not hinder them, for the kingdom of heaven belongs to such as these" (Matthew 19:14).

These words of Jesus at least indicate how much he appreciated little ones and how seriously he viewed adult and parental attitudes toward them. Grown-ups need to recognize how vulnerable children are. Parents will be wise to heed Jesus' stern warning about the dire consequences of hindering or causing a child to sin.

Bringing our children to Jesus.

> When mothers of Salem
> Their children brought to Jesus,
> The stern disciples drove them back,
> And bade them depart:
> But Jesus saw them ere they fled,
> And sweetly smiled, and kindly said,
> "Suffer little children to come unto Me."

The words of this beautiful children's hymn remind us of the importance of bringing our children to the Lord. Perhaps these "Mothers of Salem" recognized

Jesus for who he was and sensed the great opportunity of letting their children meet him. How encouraged they must have been when Jesus, despite his disciples' gruffness, welcomed the little ones and placed his hands upon them in a gesture of blessing.

The Savior's welcoming of the children should surely be an encouragement to all Christian parents to bring their children to Jesus. This may be done in a number of ways. We bring them to him in the arms of faith and prayer, asking his divine blessing and mercy to be upon them. We may also wish to do it more formally and publicly in a short service of dedication, to give thanks to God publicly and to seek the prayers of brothers and sisters in Christ on behalf of our family. This would appear to be in line with what is found in such passages as 1 Samuel 1:28; Luke 2:27, 28; and Matthew 19:13-15.

Other ways in which we bring our children to the Lord are by providing them with a suitable spirit of Christian love and nurture in our homes. Nothing can fully take the place of a godly, parental example, which might include such things as a "family altar" and instruction in the Word of God. But such influence goes beyond these. We need to offer our children the security and support of our friendship. It is not enough to drag them off to countless meetings at church. Church should have an important place in the Christian family's schedule, but it is more important to be around to explain the love of Jesus in the everyday things of life. We must also be ready to give good answers to sincere questions.

We cannot guarantee that our children will be saved nor be sure that they will grow up to live for the Lord. However, there is a sense in which we can trust our children into the safe hands of Christ, knowing that he cares as much for families as he does for individuals.

Providing wisely. "Which of you, if his son asks for bread, will give him a stone? Or if he asks for a fish, will give him a snake? If you, then, though you are evil, know how to give good gifts to your children, how much more will your Father in heaven give good gifts to those who ask him!" (Matthew 7:9-11).

Although Jesus' main lesson, in this context, is on prayer and especially on God's grace in answering, he showed also the parent's responsibility to make wise provision for his children. It is one thing to give gifts to our children; it is another thing to give them "good gifts." Our Lord implied that it is a part of parenthood to know the difference. Two extremes are to be avoided. On the one hand, we must not cheat our children; but on the other, we must not indulge them. In the above passage the two things asked for are simple items from the staple diet of the people of Galilee in the time of Jesus. In the home where Jesus grew up as a boy it is very doubtful whether there were many extras. People, whether adults or children, seemed to be content with the simple basics of life.

We get this same feeling from the story of the boy who gave his lunch to Jesus. His meal consisted of five small barley loaves and two small fish. Although Jesus multiplied the food so that it amply fed the entire multitude, we see that he made sure that there was no waste. Whatever was left over was collected and, no doubt, put to good use (John 6:8-13). How often do we spare a thought for the boy's mother who had wisely provided for her son's needs? We can be sure that Jesus not only thanked the lad but sent a word of thanks home to his mother.

By contrast, we might recall the story of the Prodigal Son. While his spending habits were without excuse, the father's giving him the money to squander leaves plenty of unanswered questions. We might also catch a hint of parental favoritism from this story; at least that was how the elder son felt.

Another parable Jesus told was about the friend who called at midnight. The details given about the man who provided the bread are worth noting. This man had obviously made provision for his family and had some to spare. He knew that all his children were in bed, where they should be at midnight, and that his house was secure against intruders. Those are good lessons for any parent to keep in mind.

CHILDREN'S CARE FOR PARENTS

It is clear, from Jesus' words spoken to the Scribes and Pharisees from Jerusalem, that he believed that the care of parents was more important than religious tradition: "And why do you break the command of God for the sake of your tradition? For God said, 'Honor your father and mother,' and, 'Anyone who curses his father and mother must be put to death.' But you say that if a man says to his father and mother, 'Whatever help you might otherwise have received from me is a gift devoted to God,' he is not to 'honor his father' with it. Thus you nullify the word of God for the sake of your tradition" (Matthew 15:3-6).

We notice a number of things from this passage. First, it is crystal clear that in quoting from the Ten Commandments Jesus accepted that they were moral and still valid to honor and provide for parents in need. Keeping them was not just an option—it was what God's moral law required. Any attempt to evade this law, even in the name of religion, was wrong as far as Jesus was concerned.

What Jesus was dealing with was the Jewish custom of "Corban." It amounted to a sort of trust arrangement whereby funds could be deposited for safe keeping in the temple treasury. They were thus available for religious purposes but could be reclaimed on demand, no doubt with a small interest, in the event of an emergency. Apparently there was the strange feeling that money on loan to God might very well secure some spiritual preferment.

Jesus saw right through this sham and taught the lesson that "religious" excuses for not supporting needy parents are no better than any other kind. In fact he infers that there are no worse shams than religious ones.

In our welfare society, we need to remember Jesus' words. Children are unworthy who fail to care for and show love to their elderly parents. Whether we are parents or children we need to remember that filial and family love and involvement are far more significant spiritually than any amount of religious profession or even involvement in Christian service and public preaching. If we have any question about the things the Lord values, his teaching here indicates that he set far more store by honesty than religious profession.

FAMILY AND SPIRITUAL LOYALTIES

Jesus warned against allowing earthly relationships to intrude on our relationship with God. He said: "If anyone comes to me and does not hate his father and mother, his wife and children, his brothers and sisters—yes, even his own life—cannot be my disciple" (Luke 14:26).

On the surface this certainly sounds like an impossible demand and might even be cited to warrant the selfish conduct referred to in the last section. However, we have a parallel passage from Matthew's Gospel which interprets Jesus' words for us: "He that loveth father or mother more than me is not worthy of me: and he that loveth son or daughter more than me is not worthy of me" (Matthew 10:37).

From Matthew we discover that the word "hate" in the context of Jesus' call to discipleship is a comparative term. It does not mean "hatred" in the sense that we think of it. Obviously that would be sin and would be condemned by Jesus (Matthew 5:21, 22).

What Jesus is saying in effect is that our love for our family must not become idolatrous nor take the place of our love for God. The time may come when relations may make demands of us which could only be met by our being disloyal to Christ. In this case the line of duty is clear. The Lord must come first.

If we find these demands of Jesus difficult, it will help if we read them in context. He is seeking to show that our commitment to him should not be frivolous or out of any sense of self-interest. His parable talked about people who lightly regarded the importance of the kingdom of God and their eternal destiny so that they used relatives as an excuse for not entering into it. For example, in the terms of the parable, there was a man who turned down the invitation to the great banquet on the basis that he had "married a wife." He made her the excuse for his own rudeness.

When Jesus said to the would-be disciple who wanted first to go home and bury his father, "Let the dead bury their dead," he was not being callous. Jesus knew that if the man's father had in fact been lying dead at home, he would not have been allowed out of the house. The Lord saw through the man's excuses. What the fellow really meant was that he would like to go home to his aged father, wait until he had died, pick up his share of the inheritance, and then he might consider becoming a disciple of Jesus. This is the kind of self-love that disqualifies us from identifying with Jesus.

Jesus' teaching is carefully balanced. On the one hand he urged care of family; but on the other he warned against allowing family or even self to intrude into the area of our commitment to God. Anyone who understands the true meaning of Christian commitment will make the most responsible parent or relative. Christianity really should begin at home.

STUDY QUESTIONS

1. What does Jesus mean when he says we must become like children?
2. Do you think Jesus' words in Matthew 18:6 support the idea of capital punishment?
3. In what ways does the "kingdom of heaven" belong to children (Matthew 19:14)?
4. What do Christian parents owe their children?
5. Suggest an "order of service" for an occasion of the dedication of children.
6. What did Jesus suggest were the responsibilities of children toward their parents?
7. How can we "love" family more than we love Christ?

PART THREE

PAUL'S TEACHING ABOUT MARRIAGE AND FAMILY

"I constantly remember you in my prayers. Recalling your tears, I long to see you, so that I may be filled with joy. I have been reminded of your sincere faith, which first lived in your grandmother Lois and in your mother Eunice and, I am persuaded, now lives in you also. For this reason I remind you to fan into flame the gift of God, which is in you through the laying on of my hands. For God did not give us a spirit of timidity, but a spirit of power, of love and of self-discipline" (2 Timothy 1:3-7).

HIS OWN FAMILY

Paul has often been called a "woman hater" or a "marriage hater," but neither label will stick if we look at the total context of his life and teaching. In fact, we shall see that Paul had a great appreciation of women, of marriage, of parenting, and of family life in general.

PAUL'S PERSONAL EXPERIENCE OF FAMILY LIFE

Although Paul said very little about his own family, a careful reading of his epistles as well as the book of Acts tells a lot about this subject. Paul's parents, although they were dispersion Jews living in the famous Cilician city of Tarsus, third city of the world of that day, were evidently keen to preserve the customs of their Jewish homeland. They spoke Aramaic in their home (this apparently is the sense of, "a Hebrew of Hebrews," Philippians 3:5); and they tried to see that their son was fluent in this language also (Acts 22:2). As believers in the Torah, they saw to it that their son was circumcised on his eighth day. Their naming him "Saul" showed not only their Benjamite pride as members of the tribe that had furnished Israel with its first king, but also their hope that their son, like his great namesake, would influence his nation for good.

When the time came for Paul's further education, his parents sent him not to the local "University of Tarsus," but to the city of Jerusalem, there to sit at the feet of the well-known teacher Gamaliel. We are not told at what age Paul was sent to Jerusalem, but it was probably quite early since he refers to having been "brought up" in that city (Acts 22:3).

Paul's father was a member of the privileged elite who could call themselves "Pharisees," a political group of Jews to which the apostle himself evidently belonged at one time (Acts 23:6). And, like all good Jewish parents, Paul's father saw to it that his son, despite his evident academic skills, learned an honest trade, that of a leatherworker or tentmaker (Acts 18:3).

Paul's mother was mentioned only once and then simply as the one who gave him birth (Galatians 1:5). She no doubt was a devout Jewess who cared for her family, sharing with them her belief in Jehovah and in the teachings of the Torah. Traditionally, Jewish mothers taught their children the alphabet and how to read from the law by the time they were five years old.

We know that Paul had a sister and a nephew who lived in Jerusalem and were close enough to him to be concerned about his safety and well-being (Acts 23:16). Although we are not told so in so many words, they were probably Christians since they, unlike the rest of his family, had chosen not to ostracize Paul but to keep in touch with him. Two other New Testament characters may have been members of Paul's family, Andronicus and Junia. Paul referred to them as "my kinsmen" and probably meant "my relatives." They were converted to Christ before Paul was and may even have held the rank of "apostle" (Romans 16:7, NIV).

Unfortunately, when Saul of Tarsus became a Christian his parents evidently disowned him. That, it is generally agreed, appears to be the sense of the apostle's words to the Philippians when he wrote, "Christ Jesus my Lord, for whose sake I have lost all things" (Philippians 3:8). He used the aorist tense, perhaps to suggest a particular time or day when he was officially disinherited. Typically Paul did not question his parents' motive. He no doubt realized that they, like himself, at one stage acted "ignorantly in unbelief" (1 Timothy 1:13). Paul would realize that in his parents' eyes his conversion to Christianity would be regarded as a defection from Judaism, a kind of betrayal.

There is no evidence that Paul ever had children of his own, which would certainly be unusual for a married Jew. Children were considered a "heritage from the Lord" (Psalm 127:3), the essential complement of any true marriage. His having no children would add pathos and meaning to his reference to Timothy as "my own son in the faith" (1 Timothy 1:2; 2 Timothy 2:1) and to his beautiful commendation of him in the epistle to the Philippians where he wrote: "I hope in the Lord Jesus to send Timothy to you soon, that I also may be cheered when I receive news about you. I have no one else like him, who takes a genuine interest in your welfare. For everyone looks out for his own interests, not those of Jesus Christ. But you know that Timothy has proved himself, because as a son with his father he has served with me in the work of the gospel" (Philippians 2:19-22).

This same feeling about Paul's spiritual children appears in his appeal on behalf of Onesimus. He wrote to Philemon: "I appeal to you for my son Onesimus, who became my son while I was in chains. Formerly he was useless to you, but now he has become useful both to you and to me" (Philemon 10, 11).

One further look at Paul's deep concern for his spiritual offspring is seen in his epistle to the Galatians. There he described his readers as, "my little children [Greek *teknia mou*], of whom I travail in birth again until Christ be formed in you" (Galatians 4:19). His metaphor combines the concern of both a mother and father. Paul seems to have been one of those rare ones who had the heart of both.

PAUL'S WIFE?

Another question which may not yet be answered is, "Did Paul have a wife?" On the one hand there are those who say yes and base their finding on the fact that Paul was probably, at one time, a member of the Sanhedrin (Acts 22:20; 26:10). Some think that all members of the Jewish Council were required to be married. However, the verses cited need not mean that Paul held official status. In any case, his youth would almost certainly preclude him from a seat in the Sanhedrin.

If it could be shown that Paul was in fact married, then the question arises, how could he write, "I wish that all men were as I am"? In context he clearly meant that he was unmarried (1 Corinthians 7:7). One suggestion is that while Paul was obviously unmarried at the time of writing the first epistle to the Corinthians (probably A.D. 57), he may have been married earlier but was now widowed. Another view is that his former wife had deserted him upon his conversion to Christ. This, it is said, accounts for his supposedly "unhappy view" of marriage in 1 Corinthians.

This is conjecture, and we must always be careful about reading things into the text. Paul certainly was not against celibacy, yet clearly defended his right to maintain and enjoy the companionship of a believing wife (1 Corinthians 9:5). Whatever may be alleged to the contrary, Paul presented a high view of marriage in 1 Corinthians 7. If there is an emphasis here it is explained by his phrase "because of the present crisis" (v. 26). Paul's point was that married people in times of persecution would have a hard time; whereas a single person had only his own skin to save.

PAUL'S APOSTOLIC AUTHORITY

Some believe, on the basis of certain statements the apostle himself made in 1 Corinthians 7, that he did not claim divine authority for his teaching. They argue that we should read Paul as merely offering finite, "occasional advice" in answer to the local and temporary problems faced by the Corinthian church. This line of reasoning serves only to cast doubt on the integrity and lasting value of Paul's counsel and to erode his authority as a writer of "inspired Scripture." After all, if we are free to ignore this or that part of the apostle's teaching because it is "temporary," "local," or "culturally related," then how can we be sure of the reliability and integrity of the rest? What is the basis upon which we can make such judgments? They certainly appear to be quite subjective.

In order to understand this statement we must study Paul's words carefully, looking both at what appears to be negative statements and at his positive claims: "I say this as a concession, not as a command" (1 Corinthians 7:6). The King James Version translation of this verse is "I speak this by permission, and not of commandment." This rather misleading translation makes Paul sound as though he is saying that he is permitted but not commanded by the Lord to give this advice. In fact the apostle was not speaking of his receiving permission but of his giving it to others! This sense is well expressed in the New International Version rendering, "I say this as a concession, not as a command."

Bearing this in mind, we see that this verse must be considered as underlining Paul's authority. A man who writes thus to a Christian church obviously senses more than human inspiration.

Two other such verses are "To the rest I say this (I, not the Lord)" (v. 12); and "I have no command from the Lord, but I give a judgment as one who by the Lord's mercy is trustworthy" (v. 25). Here Paul was not suggesting that what he wrote was different from what the Lord said. Nor was he suggesting that what follows was his own rather than the Lord's counsel. His point was that whereas in some cases he could cite a specific statement made by Christ—in this instance he could not. Thus his statement had no immediate bearing on the relative or absolute inspiration of his own words. In fact, his words serve only to support that the apostle wrote under a sense of divine inspiration. Otherwise he would have been reluctant to label his words as "trustworthy," which would have been quite out of keeping with what we know of Paul's character.

In another passage Paul wrote, "To the married I give this command (not I, but the Lord): A wife must not separate from her husband." Here Paul showed no reluctance about divine authority but backed up his statements with a specific quotation from Jesus. When he wrote, "Let not the wife depart from her husband," Paul believed that he was simply giving the teaching of Jesus found in its summary form in the Sermon on the Mount (Mark 10:6-12; Matthew 19:4-9).

Paul's statement in verse 17, "This is the rule I lay down in all the churches," certainly has the ring of authority about it. Who except an apostle, sensing divine inspiration, would write thus? This does not seem to be an arbitrary, human opinion but a command bearing the stamp of the Lord Jesus. Paul's statement, "I am saying this for your own good, not to restrict you. I want to live in a right way in undivided devotion to the Lord" (v. 35), must surely have been to confirm his sense of divine direction. He is saying, in effect, "If you follow my advice it will be for your spiritual good and you will be living in the right way before God."

Whatever we may think about Paul's teaching on marriage and human relationships, we must accept that he saw himself as offering authoritative, divinely inspired statements. To deny this is not only to misunderstand Paul but also to question the total authority of Scripture.

STUDY QUESTIONS

1. What things in Paul's background did he consider advantages?
2. Consider all the New Testament references to Paul's family.
3. Why was it so difficult for Paul's parents to accept his conversion to Christ?
4. Was Paul a champion of celibacy?
5. In what ways did Paul express his apostolic authority?
6. On what grounds had Paul been considered as being against women or marriage?
7. What were Paul's reasons for saying that people should remain unmarried? How relevant are these reasons today?

PAUL'S PRINCIPLES CONCERNING MARRIAGE

Paul's direct teaching on marriage is found mainly in four of his epistles: 1 Corinthians, Ephesians, 1 and 2 Timothy, and Titus. As we might expect, his emphasis in each context was slightly different, but his principles remained the same throughout.

THE DIVINE INSTITUTION OF MARRIAGE

Like his Master before him, Paul based the validity of marriage on God's order in creation. For him, marriage was not the result of man's social evolution nor a matter of human convenience, but a gift from God. Paul wrote: "For this reason a man will leave his father and mother and be united to his wife, and they will become one flesh" (Genesis 2:24).

Whatever Paul said about marriage was conditioned on his sense of its divine origin. Whether he himself was married, whether he believed that some Christians were called to a life of celibacy, or whether under some circumstances Paul permitted divorce are all incidental to his basic premise that marriage was instituted by God.

THE SANCTITY OF MARRIAGE

There was nothing secular in Paul's view of marriage. For him marriage was based on divine revelation, involved a solemn covenant, and demanded absolute fidelity. In other words, it was sacred in every part.

Paul spoke also about the sanctity of marriage in the context of mixed relationships. He wrote, "For the unbelieving husband has been sanctified through his wife, and the unbelieving wife has been sanctified through her believing husband. Otherwise your children would be unclean, but as it is, they are holy" (1 Corinthians 7:14).

He appeared to be talking about a convert to Christ who was planning to leave his or her still-unsaved spouse. Perhaps the convert was wondering whether staying in the marriage which was contracted in his or her pre-Christian days was bringing some sort of shame on the name of Christ, or if there was something unholy about it. "On the contrary," said Paul. "Conversion to Christ cannot be made an excuse for desertion or divorce. You must stay, remembering that marriage does not depend on your being a Christian or a pagan."

It would seem that for Paul even a non-Christian marriage was to be regarded as within the framework of God's ordinance. To deny this is not only to threaten human society but also the destiny of our children. Christianity confirms rather than destroys normal and proper human relationships.

Paul saw a special blessing resting upon the partner and offspring of a believer, whether or not the former appreciated it. When Paul said that the unbelieving spouse is "sanctified" and the children are "holy," he was not saying that a Christian's faith saves his family also. He was simply saying that to be related to a Christian, be it spouse or parent, sets the unsaved ones apart for blessing and makes them the very special subject of prayer and evangelism (1 Corinthians 7:16). Marriage itself should cement the bonds of human family relationships.

Paul gave his clearest statement about the sanctity of marriage when he compared the relationship of husband and wife to that between Christ and the Church. He wrote: "This is a profound mystery—but I am talking about Christ and the church" (Ephesians 5:32). Christian marriage is a visualization of the ideal relationship existing between Christ and his Church. Nothing could be more sacred in terms of marital relationships.

THE PERMANENCE OF MARRIAGE
For Paul, marriage was considered to be a permanent relationship. Unlike other human contracts, Christian marriage must not be entered into with written-in "escape clauses." Whatever certain contemporary church groups may decide, marriage "is for keeps." We are not here discussing the vexing question of divorce, nor the so-called "Pauline privilege clause." We are looking at God-given ideals.

Several statements in 1 Corinthians give us the principles:

"To the married I give this command (not I, but the

Lord): A wife must not separate from her husband"
(1 Corinthians 7:10).

"A husband must not divorce his wife" (v. 11).

"If any brother has a wife who is not a believer and she is willing to live with him, he must not divorce her" (v. 12).

"She must not divorce him" (v. 13).

"Are you married? Do not seek a divorce" (v. 27).

"A woman is bound to her husband as long as he lives" (v. 39).

It will be helpful to look at the situations Paul mentioned in these verses, remembering also that here he was answering questions posed by his Christian friends at Corinth. First, the apostle was answering the query of the new convert to Christ who wondered if celibacy might be more honorable than marriage. Paul's answer was "No!" (vv. 10, 11, 27).

There was also the new Christian who wondered whether he or she should dissolve his now "mixed marriage" (vv. 12, 13). Again Paul's answer was a "No!" Paul made it plain that marriage was to be regarded as a life long relationship (v. 39; see also Romans 7:2).

In writing to the Ephesians, Paul compared "leaving" with "cleaving" (Ephesians 5:31). The one must be as much a matter of commitment as the other. There can be nothing tentative about either if there is to be harmony in marriage. Paul used the same word as Jesus to explain the idea of a close, continuing union. Any doubt of what Paul meant about the permanence of marriage is explained by his analogy of leaving and cleaving. The marriage between a man and his wife should be permanent, like the bond between Christ and his Church.

THE EXCLUSIVENESS OF MARRIAGE

The same verses which express Paul's feelings about the sacredness and permanence of marriage point to its exclusiveness (1 Corinthians 7). Paul was clear in his beliefs about monogamy and fidelity in marriage. Just as marriage is an intensely inclusive relationship based on perfect union between husband and wife, so is it an exclusive relationship. All others are excluded from the inner intimacies and physical relationships of marriage.

Polygamy was viewed as an aberration not only by Paul but also by Christ, since they both based their teachings on the original creation order stated in Genesis 2:24. This basic verse as clearly forbids polygamy as it affirms monogamy. It speaks of a man's being united to his wife, not to his *wives* nor to his concubines. It speaks of two people, a man and his wife, becoming one flesh.

Paul wrote: "Each one of you also must love his wife as he loves himself" (Ephesians 5:33).

It seems that Paul wanted to be quite specific for his male readers. Whatever the outside world was doing and saying, love for any other than one's own wife was immorality and a violation of God's ideal.

Again when Paul was discussing the qualifications for church leadership and Christian service, he said that a man should be "the husband of one wife" (1 Timothy 3:2, 12; Titus 1:6). Some wonder if Paul meant to exclude the polygamous man, or the divorced man, or whether he was simply saying that the only man qualified for leadership in the church was the "one-woman-kind-of-man." Since it is doubtful that polygamy was a serious problem in Paul's day, the latter is probably what he meant. Paul was saying that if a man didn't accept the sanctity

of marriage he was disqualified for leadership
(1 Timothy 5:9).

In support of Paul's idea of the exclusiveness of
marriage we might cite all his writings to command
purity and to condemn immorality (Romans 13:13;
1 Corinthians 5:1-13; 6:9, 13, 15-20; 10:8-13;
Galatians 5:19-21; Ephesians 5:3; Colossians 3:5;
1 Thessalonians 4:3-8; 1 Timothy 5:2).

THE BEAUTY OF MARRIAGE

To Paul, marriage was a picture of the relationship
between Christ and his Church. We see his emphasis
on the beauty of the marriage bond. He described
Christ's purpose for the Church as being "to make
her holy, cleansing her by the washing with water
through the word, and to present her to himself as a
radiant church, without stain or wrinkle or any other
blemish, but holy and blameless." Paul then added:
"In this same way, husbands ought to love their
wives" (Ephesians 5:25-28). Just as the Church is the
glorious complement of Christ, so should the bride be
of her bridegroom.

Paul described marriage as something more than
a contractual arrangement between two consenting
partners. Rather it is the beginning of the most
beautiful relationship that two human beings in love
can enjoy.

STUDY QUESTIONS

1. Examine Paul's idea of the sanctity of marriage.
2. Why did Paul counsel Christians to remain
married?

3. Consider Paul's teaching as a sound basis for monogamy.

4. What in Paul's view gave marriage its special spiritual dimensions?

5. What lessons can married couples learn from Christ's relationship to the Church?

6. What does Paul mean in 1 Corinthians 7:14b?

7. Do you think Paul changed his mind on marriage?

CHAPTER ELEVEN

PAUL SPEAKS TO HUSBANDS AND WIVES

In an age where unisex is promoted more and more, we should remember Paul's teaching. Husbands and wives are equal partners in grace, though their roles and responsibilities are as diverse as their genders. Some today base their beliefs about equality in marriage on the apostle's words: "There is neither Jew nor Greek, slave nor free, *male nor female,* for you are all one in Christ Jesus" (Galatians 3:28). Such an idea is a misunderstanding which makes nonsense of Paul's teaching in 1 Corinthians and the pastoral letters.

In this passage Paul was explaining that because of our acceptance in Christ, the things which determine one's acceptance, race, social status, and gender, had all been removed. His point was that the blessing of being right with God is available to all on the basis of faith in Christ. Our standing in grace does not now depend on whether we are Jew or Greek, slave or freeman, man or woman. However, this standing does not suddenly remove social and sexual distinctions.

Christians are still seen as being men or women, and this fact was clearly reckoned with in Paul's teaching in relation to the local church and to marriage.

THE HUSBAND'S RESPONSIBILITIES

He is a leader. Paul wrote: "Now I want you to realize that the head of every man is Christ, and the head of the woman is man, and the head of Christ is God" (1 Corinthians 11:3).

This Scripture verse clearly suggests that whether he likes it or not, a husband is called to be a godly leader in his home, not to be a dictator nor a despot, but a loving guide who accepts responsibility for the direction of his home. A Christian husband may shrink from headship unless he remembers that it is part of his obedience to Christ, his Lord.

Paul's teaching shows us that the husband's headship has nothing to do with value judgments. The man is in no sense superior to his wife. This is clear from the apostle's reference to Christ's relationship to the Father. God is the head of Christ not in the sense of being superior or prior to him, but in the sense that Christ accepts his role of revealer and Savior in submission to the Father. If we remember this, our role is easier to accept. Paul's words further confirm this: "For the husband is the head of the wife as Christ is the head of the church, his body, of which he is the Savior" (Ephesians 5:23).

This acceptance of a responsible leadership role is important in the Christian home, as Paul's guidelines for elders and deacons show (1 Timothy 3). Not all Christian husbands are called to church leadership, but since all may desire this "noble task," the requirements apply to all men in the church.

According to Paul, a man should "Manage his own family well and see that his children obey him with proper respect" (1 Timothy 3:4). The measure of man's spiritual stature depends very much on his acceptance of his leadership role in his marriage and home.

He Is a Lover. Some "macho types" need to realize that there can be no leadership without love. In the very context where Paul talked about the husband's headship, he mentioned the responsibility of the man to love his wife. Paul had much more to say about the husband's duty to love than about his duty to lead. He wrote: "Husbands love your wives, just as Christ loved the church and gave himself up for her to make her holy. . . . In this same way, husbands ought to love their wives as their own bodies. . . . Each one of you also must love his wife as he loves himself" (Ephesians 5:25, 28, 33).

Paul's teaching was clear. The pattern for the husband's love for his wife is to be that of Christ. Just as Christ's love selected his heavenly bride, led him to sacrifice himself for her, and leads him to be concerned about her present and eternal blessing, so should a husband's love be offered selflessly for his wife. Such standards are high, but Paul was talking about Christian marriage.

A Christian husband's love will not be mere sentiment but will be practical, considerate, and kind. Writing to the Colossians, Paul urged, "Husbands love your wives and do not be harsh with them" (Colossians 3:19). The apostle, speaking quite frankly, said: "The husband should fulfill his marital duty to his wife, and likewise the wife to her husband. The wife's body does not belong to her alone but also to her husband. In the same way, the husband's body does not belong to him alone but also to his wife" (1 Corinthians 7:3, 4).

Paul was pointing out that both husband and wife have duties to fulfill in the physical side of marriage. Neither must withold sexual fulfillment from the other except for some mutually accepted reason; and even then, only for a short time. The governing factor in all this would be love.

There are far more exhortations to the husband to love his wife than the wife to love the husband. Paul evidently recognized that Christian husbands must understand that their wives have a deep need to be loved and to be secure in the expression of their husbands' love. It is not difficult for a wife who is secure in her husband's love to submit to his leadership. She will feel no threat to her womanhood nor any erosion of her spiritual authority as a fulfilled Christian wife.

He is a Provider. Paul wrote to the husband: "He who loves his wife loves himself. After all, no one ever hated his own body, but he feeds and cares for it, just as Christ does the church—for we are members of his body" (Ephesians 5:28-30).

The apostle wrote also: "If anyone does not provide for his relatives, and especially for his immediate family, he has denied the faith and is worse than an unbeliever" (1 Timothy 5:8).

Whatever else Paul was saying, he was teaching that in a Christian marriage the husband's duty is to be a provider. However strange this may sound, in a two-income, working-wife society, we do well to give Paul's teaching careful thought. Certainly such an idea may affect our affluence and limit our resources, but it might very well increase our dependence on God and therefore our spirituality. In any case, even Scripture seems to recognize that poverty is more congenial to saintliness than affluence (1 Timothy 6:6-10).

Now while this *providing* seems to suggest material needs, it includes much more. Paul's words "nourish" and "cherish" convey the ideas of *nurturing, bringing up,* and *protecting from harm.* Such picture words remind the Christian husband that as he cares for and protects his own life, so he must exercise the same concern for his wife, who is in fact an integral part of him. Self-interest, independency, or competition are all destructive to marital harmony. A husband who doesn't want to provide for, or who fails to protect his wife against other people, sometimes even including her children, has not fully understood his duties. A wife who demands the right to her own income, or who is extravagant, or who questions her husband's ability or right in this matter, is not helping cement marriage bonds.

Even though these are difficult times economically, the poor in our country today are rich compared to those in Paul's day. Perhaps the trouble is that we expect too much. We tend to consider luxuries as necessities, and we take it for granted that we have an inalienable right to "keep up with the Joneses." Many newly married couples seem to think they should start off at the level their parents have reached. It is all too easy to forget that their parents struggled and made personal sacrifice on behalf of these very offspring who now demand so much.

It is not only young people who want affluence. Many "mature" Christian men make the mistake of pursuing promotion and money at the risk of sacrificing their involvement with their families and their usefulness in the local church. We need to relearn the lesson Paul taught by his life and letters, that it really takes very little of material things to be happy and content (Philippians 4:11).

THE WIFE'S RESPONSIBILITIES

She Is a Supporter. However difficult or demeaning she may regard it, the Christian wife is called to submit to her husband's leadership. Of course, if a husband loves his wife and leads her according to the pattern set by Christ, it will not be hard for the wife to follow. Paul wrote: "Submit to one another out of reverence for Christ. Wives, submit to your husbands as to the Lord. For the husband is the head of the wife as Christ is the head of the church, his body, of which he is Savior. Now as the church submits to Christ, so also wives should submit to their husbands in everything" (Ephesians 5:21-24).

Paul's teaching is clear and authoritative. It would be wrong to dismiss it as out of date or to suggest that it reflects that Paul was against marriage, or that it was only a cultural practice. Paul's words are as much Scripture as any other part and should be received as such.

Paul was not saying that the wife's submission is something the husband demands, but rather something the wife gives. What is required of the Christian husband and of the wife are both gifts given. One is loving concern and leadership. The other is support and submission. Submission is a reflection of strength, not weakness, and in no way suggests that the wife is inferior. It is the mark of the dignity of her Christian womanhood that she express her submission to the Lordship of Christ by accepting her husband's leadership. Submission has nothing to do with that silly, mealy-mouthed attitude which simply says, "Yes, dear!"

One of the clever lies of our culture is that it pictures a Christian wife's submission as meaning subjugation. The truth remains that Christianity and the Bible have done more to emancipate women than anything else. Any system that teaches that a woman should not be submissive in her role as wife is clearly not Christian.

Submission in this Christian marriage context includes "making submissions." A husband who thinks he has all the answers and that the truth will die with him obviously knows nothing about leadership and less about submission to Christ, who is his Head. By the same token, a wife who encourages her husband and refuses to downgrade him will reap great benefits. Loving support will do more for a husband and for a marriage than will constant challenge. A wife will lose something of her importance and womanliness if she insists on "wearing the pants." The dominating wife, by eroding her husband's leadership, may very well lose the strong man she will one day need. It is also true that a domineering wife breeds disobedient offspring.

She Is a Homemaker. In his pastoral letters Paul spoke about the importance of wives as homemakers. He wrote: "Then they [older women] can train the younger women to love their husbands and children, to be self-controlled and pure, to be busy at home, to be kind, and to be subject to their husbands, so that no one will malign the word of God" (Titus 2:4, 5).

While the husband has the duty to provide, it is the

wife who has to be a good steward of what is provided—that is, in the home. Women have that special ability for making a house into a home, and there is certainly nothing demeaning about that. There is no more noble calling than to be a wife and mother. How many godly, hospitable, contented wives and mothers have made deep impressions for good on their families and on society! If there is an economic need or if a woman feels frustrated through her being unable to use her talents or compete in the world, then there are still vast opportunities open to her in terms of working at home. There are today, as in the apostle's day, quite a number of cottage crafts and industries and there are many people who prefer these handmade products to the shoddy, mass-produced alternatives. Furthermore, there are many church-related and Christian service opportunities open to wives who have time on their hands. If it is busyness or the fulfillment of activity that women need, then they are limited only by their creative abilities.

A wife who is contented, kind, industrious, thrifty, organized, and hospitable is a blessing to any husband and family and is worth her weight in gold. Such a woman is not likely to bring the Word of God into disrepute. Paul certainly appreciated the importance of Christian wives and mothers (2 Timothy 1:5; Romans 16:13). Bible-believing people, who fully understand Paul's writing, will appreciate them too.

STUDY QUESTIONS
1. How do you understand Paul's teaching about "headship" in 1 Corinthians 11?

2. How does Scripture's demand that a husband "love" his wife control his exercise of leadership?

3. What are the "domestic criteria" for Christian leadership?

4. How does a "two-income" family practically interpret Paul's idea of the husband as the breadwinner?

5. How does a Christian wife's submission guard against her husband's domination?

6. What are the blessings of being a homemaker?

PAUL
ON THE FAMILY

Although Paul was not a parent, his teachings to parents are important: "Children, obey your parents in the Lord, for this is right. Honor your father and mother—which is the first commandment with a promise—that it may go well with you and that you may enjoy long life on the earth. Fathers, do not exasperate your children; instead, bring them up in the training and instruction of the Lord" (Ephesians 6:1-4).

Christian parents are exhorted by Paul to be concerned about four things: obedience, nurture, admonition, and love (Ephesians 6:4; 1 Timothy 3:4). Each is like an essential ingredient in a recipe for domestic and family happiness. It is sad that so many well-intentioned Christian parents have ill-treated their children. By pandering to their children's whims, these parents thought they were being kind. In being indulgent they have ended up producing self-centered offspring who have not only broken their parents' hearts but have wrought havoc in the church.

OBEDIENCE

Considerable emphasis is placed in Scripture on obedience, obedience to God and the obedience of children to earthly parents. On the surface, Paul's teaching in Ephesians 6:4 looked like a command to believing children; and of course, it is: "[the overseer must] manage his own family well and see that his children obey him with proper respect" (1 Timothy 3:4).

Obedience must be required by Christian parents. Through learning to obey a child learns about authority, law, responsibility, and submission to God. It is sad when Christian parents fail to instill obedience into the minds of their children. Not only will they themselves, and their children, suffer—but so will the church and society in general.

Paul very wisely inserted a balance both in Ephesians 6:4 and in Colossians 3:21. In the latter passage he wrote, "Fathers do not embitter your children or they will become discouraged." We exasperate or embitter our children if we require their obedience without explanation. We also do it by constantly nagging them or by making idle and empty threats. Many Christian parents have lost their children's respect either by being too demanding or too soft. There is a happy medium in this matter, as in so many other things in life. An absentee father who is too busy to spend time with his children, or too obsessed with his own "ladder climbing" to listen to their conversation, need not be surprised if he rears irresponsible and disobedient children. Similarly a mother who refuses to accept her role in the home and challenges her husband's leadership is unlikely to raise obedient children.

Notice that Paul addressed his words to "fathers."

Did he do this because it is the father's responsibility to direct the family? Or did he realize how much shorter tempered and less patient fathers are inclined to be than mothers? Probably for both reasons. Perhaps he had suffered irreparable harm through his own religious, Pharisee father who may have made quite unreasonable demands upon young Saul. There are still fathers who seem to be more anxious to prove some ridiculous and unimportant point of religion than to win their children for Christ by their firm, but gracious, personal conduct.

Christian fathers will better appreciate their duty if they remember that the Bible teaches that God as Father is the pattern for human parents. This is the point of Paul's words to the Ephesians: "For this cause I kneel before the Father, from whom his whole family [patria] in heaven and on earth derives its name" (Ephesians 3:14, 15). This, of course, is precisely opposite to the current view which says that the idea of God as Father is a projection of our innate father consciousness.

Clearly this truth from the Bible is as challenging as it is sensible. It reminds fathers that, to some degree, their children's idea of God is conditioned by what they see in their own earthly father. What a tragedy that the only concept some children have of God as Father is the one they have learned from a promiscuous and drunken parent! Surely such people have a lot to answer for. As the strange proverb puts it: "The parents have eaten sour grapes and have set their children's teeth on edge" (Ezekiel 18:2).

It is interesting to note that Paul bases his call for obedience on four things: the Lordship of Christ; normal family ethics; the Decalogue; and the good pleasure of Christ.

The Lordship of Christ. By using the phrase, "in the Lord," Paul showed the focus of his teaching. He was talking about homes that were under the Lordship of Christ. He was not merely teaching general ethics but Christian ethics. Some wonder if Paul was writing to Christian children whose parents may not, in fact, have been Christians. He was telling them that part of their commitment to Christ was to obey their parents. Or, was Paul reminding the children of Christian parents that their special privilege as members of a Christian household requires their obedience? Others question whether or not Paul was advising children to obey only insofar as their parents' commands do not conflict with God's requirements. To put it another way, what does a Christian child do, particularly a teenager, should his parents tell him to do something which he believes is contrary to Scripture? These are all interesting questions and no doubt might all be included under the general heading "in the Lord."

In the light of the context, and the quotation from the Ten Commandments, it would seem that Paul was writing in more general terms to Christian parents and their children. He was saying that in a Christian home every thought and action should be governed by faith in Christ. Certainly he was not limiting obedience to Christian children. Children are capable of learning to obey from a very early age just as they are capable of understanding the words, "Jesus loves me." Parents who themselves love the Lord Jesus and have surrendered their own wills to him find it easy to teach their children to obey. They are right to teach their children that such obedience is required of them if for no other reason than that they are members of a Christian family. This instruction applies to teenagers as it does to infants, although how it is applied will vary and require grace and growing skills in parental guidance.

Normal Family Ethics. Paul's second ground for filial obedience was because "this is right *[dikaion]*." The word "right" sometimes translated "just" or "righteous," has in it the idea of "conformity to a standard." Paul based his argument for Christian conduct on Scripture, or what we may call "supernatural revelation." He also appealed to natural instinct, or conventional morality. After all, most societies, Christian or otherwise, recognize the value of children obeying their parents and of parents acting responsibly toward their children. Such conduct appears "right" in pagan as well as Christian eyes. Most ethnic groups have their built-in code of family ethics, if only to preserve the culture of that group.

The Decalogue. Paul's third reason for why children should obey is the fifth of the Ten Commandments, which makes it clear the standard Paul had in mind. Having been reared in a Jewish home, Paul saw the value of living according to God's law. He saw also that its moral aspect was still valid. Quoting the law, Paul wrote: "Honor your father and mother— which is the first commandment with a promise—that it may go well with you, and that you may enjoy long life on the earth" (Deuteronomy 5:16).

Quite apart from the incentives he noted, Paul saw that this great law applied also to Christians. When he spoke of the primacy of his commandment he was reminding his readers that, in a sense, parents are God's vice-regents in the home and, as such, are to be obeyed. It is likely that Paul was reminding his readers that while long life may be a "fringe benefit" of children obeying parents, it is clear that any society which accepts God's standards as the basis of its ethics for the family is more likely to survive. Any student of history will agree that when there is a breakdown of family life, there is a breakdown of society.

Pleasing the Lord. In Colossians 3:20 Paul said that a child's obedience to his parents pleases the Lord. This is akin to his phrase in Ephesians 6:1 but does include an additional dimension. A child, especially one in a Christian home, will not find this too hard to believe. After all, the Lord Jesus was once a child whose life was an example of submission and obedience in his home at Nazareth (Luke 2:51). Let children be taught that when they obey their parents they are obeying the Savior and making him happy. To refuse to obey is to reject both the precept and example of Jesus, which is serious indeed.

NURTURE
Paul also required fathers to "nurture their children." This ancient word, "nurture," comes from *paideia,* which is also rendered, "training," "discipline," and "instruction." It suggests discipline, correction, or even "chastening." "Nurture" in this context implies the active training of a child in what we might call Christian conduct.

Such a word reminds parents of the importance of knowing for themselves what the Bible teaches as norms of conduct. How the Christian should behave is found in the Scriptures rather than in the psychology books (Paul's word, *kuriou,* "of the Lord" qualifies both his words *paideia* and *nouthesia*). Christian parents, while loving and appreciating them, will be wise to recognize that even their children (like themselves) have fallen, sinful natures. As one old preacher said as he held a new baby in his arms: "What a beautiful bundle of iniquity!"

While Paul's word may not be used to support the harsh breaking of a child's stubborn will, it may include the bending of that will. Was Paul thinking of the words of the psalm: "I will instruct you and teach you. . . . Do not be like the horse or as the mule, which have no understanding but must be controlled by bit and bridle" (Psalm 32:8, 9)?

If this is true of adults, how much more so of children. The psalmist's words remind us that just as the bit in a horse's mouth restrains it, at the same time it gives the animal freedom to be useful. Similarly discipline enables a child to discover patterns of authority and responsibility as well as acceptable behavior. The nurture of the Lord might well include, in Paul's thought, the offering of Christian guidelines and even the setting of limits. Wise as he was, Paul understood that wise young people, despite their protests, appreciate the freedom that limits provide. Young people will understand, and, sooner or later appreciate, honest Christian parents who try to act out of a sense of concern and love. Obviously it takes great parental skill to impose guidelines and then gradually to relax control as children mature.

Paul's word *paideia* emphasizes active training in contrast with *nouthesia,* which means "instruction" or "admonition." Paul may also have had the disciplines of punishment in mind. The concept of *paideia* as punishment, even corporal punishment, is never far from the surface in Scripture. Whether Paul wrote Hebrews or not is still open to discussion, but the book certainly reflects his way of thinking. In Hebrews 12:5-11 the writer cited Proverbs to show that as earthly parents are expected to punish their children to correct them, so God will chasten and even "scourge" his "sons."

This passage teaches several important truths about the discipline of children. First, it is a discipline born of love and relationship (v. 8). Second, it is natural and in order since everyone undergoes discipline. Third, true discipline teaches respect and submission to authority (v. 9). Fourth, discipline must be administered thoughtfully and never in a fit of temper: "Our fathers disciplined us for a little while as they thought best" (v. 10). The King James Version's translation, "after their own pleasure," tends to give the wrong idea, as if the fathers got their "jollies" out of beating up on the kids! Finally, discipline, while it is intended as a punishment (v. 9), must always be corrective and productive (vv. 10, 11).

Although Paul had himself suffered many physical beatings in the name of religion (2 Corinthians 11:23, 24), he nowhere supports cruelty to children nor to anyone else. People who see something sadistic or unkind in the biblical commands to mete out corporal punishment have missed the point. Christian parents must be consistent, avoid empty threats, avoid emotional reactions of temper, utterly renounce any spirit of vindictiveness or resentment, and always act wisely and out of love. There are all kinds of ways to discipline. We should avoid the approach that says, "For that you can go and read the Bible for half an hour!" or, "Now you'll have to go to the prayer meeting!" Why should we associate those things with pain or unpleasantness?

INSTRUCTION

Paul's third requirement of parents was that they bring up their children in the "admonition" of the Lord. The word "admonition" translates "*nouthesia*," which has as its roots *nous* meaning "mind," and *tithemi:* "to place." The idea therefore is to instruct or teach the mind. If "nurture" has to do with action and example, then "admonition" has to do with words and precepts.

The apostle's own Hebrew upbringing and training under the precepts of the Torah had no doubt convinced him of the importance of parents teaching their children. Like Timothy, his son in the faith, Paul had no doubt known the "sacred writings from infancy" (2 Timothy 3:15). It was this knowledge that had held him like an anchor through all his career. Writing from experience, Paul passed on this good advice to parents (2 Timothy 1:3).

Like the "nurture" he had already required, Paul said that this parental training was to be "of the Lord." Whatever else this phrase may mean, it includes the need for Christian parents to offer their children spiritual instruction and guidance. Children should be taught about God and the wonder of his great self-disclosure in the incarnation. They should be encouraged to read, study, and memorize the Scriptures. If this was important and necessary in Paul's day, how much more so in ours. Parents must offer their children a clear understanding of the basis and applications of Christian morality. They are wise parents who, like Eunice, share their faith in Christ with their children (2 Timothy 1:5). Parents who neglect this advice of Paul's or even delegate their children's spiritual training to others run the risk of grief and heartache both for themselves and their children. The moral values, the sexual perversion and propaganda, and the filth seen in the media can destroy our children and our families. The careful and diligent Christian training of our children is the only antidote for these poisons.

While verbal instruction is a part of this training, so is parental example. Christian morality is as much "caught" as "taught." Lazy, unreliable, immodest, untruthful, discourteous, untidy, indisciplined parents breed those kinds of children. There will be times when we make mistakes, but our children will accept them and still trust us, if they know that we are good and honest. In any case there is nothing wrong with apologizing to our family when we know we are wrong. We may feel we lose face momentarily, but we will gain respect ultimately. Paul knew what he was talking about. He set such store by parental guidance that he disqualified those who fail in this area, from church leadership (1 Timothy 3:4, 5, 12; Titus 1:6).

LOVE

Christian parents were urged to *love* their children. Writing to Titus, Paul said that the Christian women were to "train the younger women to love their husbands and children" (Titus 2:4). It appears strange to command it, for it seems a mother's love for her children should be instinctive. However, Paul knew his people well. Child abuse was common in the ancient world. In a society that worshiped physical strength and practiced flagrant immorality, children tended to be regarded as unproductive inconveniences.

It was here that Christian parents could be different. "Let them," said Paul, in so many words, "show that they love and appreciate their children." His Jewish background and religious training with its regard for children as "a heritage from the Lord" (Psalm 127:3), was showing through again. Be that as it may, we must remember that one of the unique features of Christianity is the value it places on children.

If Paul's words sound old-fashioned and strangely irrelevant to some modern, Christian parents, then let them consider the following. Nothing cements family relationships like parental love. Love is much more important than wealth, education, and all those status symbols so many parents crave for themselves and their children. Love is the catalyst without which nothing really happens in a home. There can be no true discipline where there is no love. Children whose parents give them everything but love are poor indeed. Children who are raised in a home where love is shown will grow up to be secure adults, better able to cope with the pressures of life.

How many unthinking parents, even some who are Christians, offer their children things, and "bought pleasures," instead of giving of themselves and their time. Children need the care and loving support of their parents, not just "pacifier handouts," and baby-sitters. The keys of your understanding heart are so much more important than those of the family car. Taking time to do things together may be demanding, especially for ambitious, acquisitive parents; but it will be rewarding in every way. Put it any way you want: "The family that plays together, like the family

that prays together, is the family that stays together."
It is sad to see families treat their homes like
restaurants where they occasionally meet to eat, or
like a dormitory in which they all have beds.

Paul obviously saw the needs of the family and was
inspired to speak to them in words that are still
relevant and useful. We can dismiss them as the
ranting of a fanatic, the counsels of a woman hater,
or of a crusty old bachelor; but if we do, and then try
to build a Christian home or family without listening,
we will fail. For Paul, Christianity begins at home,
and a great number of happy families agree.

STUDY QUESTIONS

1. Why was Paul's teaching about children such an
advance on contemporary thought?
2. Why should children be taught and required to
obey?
3. How can parental demands aggravate rather than
encourage children?
4. What do you think Paul means by the phrase "in
the Lord" in Ephesians 6:1?
5. How would you explain "pleasing the Lord" to a
child who is rebellious?
6. In what ways can parents "nurture" their
teenagers?
7. Suggest ways in which parents can say "No" to
their children.
8. What are the most important things you learned
from your parents?

PAUL'S TEACHING CONFIRMED BY PETER

We have very little detail about Peter's family and household, but we have enough to arouse our curiosity. Peter and his brother Andrew lived at Capernaum, beside the Sea of Galilee, and made their living as fishermen. While Andrew was the dreamer type, Peter was more practical and down to earth. We discover that it was through Andrew's being a disciple of John the Baptist that he met Jesus; he later introduced his brother Peter to Jesus. Later on, both men were called into the service of the Savior, and at that point left the fishing fleet on Galilee (Luke 5:8-11).

We are not told whether Andrew was married. Peter was, and it appeared that he and his wife provided a home for both Andrew and Peter's wife's mother. In fact, it was in connection with the healing of Peter's mother-in-law that Jesus visited the home in Capernaum (Mark 1:29-31). While the details of the story are sparse, we gather that there was a real spirit of caring and concern in this family. Faced with his mother-in-law's illness, Peter took the problem to Jesus. Jesus, in turn, not only healed the woman but enjoyed her spontaneous hospitality. Peter's wife remained anonymous; but reading between the lines, she was well known among the apostles and probably traveled with her husband in his later ministry (1 Corinthians 9:5). Some measure of Peter's appreciation of her can perhaps be deduced from his counsel to wives in 1 Peter: "Wives, in the same way be submissive to your husbands so that, if any of them do not believe the word, they may be won over without talk by the behavior of their wives, when they see the purity and reverence of your lives" (1 Peter 3:1, 2).

To this short but informative portion of Scripture we owe one of the most beautiful descriptions of the relationship of husbands and wives, whom Peter described as being "heirs with you of the gracious gift of life" (3:7). Whatever else this description means, it reminds us of how the two complement each other in marriage. If the reference is to physical life, then it says that a man and his wife together have the great privilege of reproducing human life. If, on the other hand, the reference is to spiritual life in Christ, then it is a reminder of the beautiful oneness that exists in Christian marriage.

COUNSEL TO WIVES

Peter, like Paul, suggested that the wife's role in marriage is that of a follower and supporter. Again, this does not demean womanhood nor make any value judgment. Peter was simply pointing to the importance of accepting proper roles in marriage. He cited both biblical and patriarchal support for his case, suggesting it was the ground of both domestic blessing (v. 1) and personal security (v. 6).

Peter continued: "Your beauty should not come from outward adornment, such as braided hair and the wearing of gold jewelry and fine clothes. Instead, it should be that of your inner self, the unfading beauty of a gentle and quiet spirit, which is of great worth in God's sight" (1 Peter 3:3, 4).

We shall probably be wise to read Peter's words about the relative importance of "outward adornment" against the background of the extravagance of the times. In the wealthier circles of Roman society, there was an almost obscene obsession with fashionable clothes, elaborate coiffures, and expensive jewelry. There is always the danger that women, or men for that matter, bereft of any real purpose in life and bored by materialism's shallow pleasures, may become self-indulgent and corrupt. No doubt it was this that Peter had in mind. Peter was not banning the reasonable use of stylish clothes nor even moderate use of cosmetics. He was just trying to redress the balance, reminding his readers that beauty of character and purity of conduct must take priority over making a wasteful show in our dress. Whether men or women, we do well to ask ourselves whether we are more concerned to make an impression on men or on God.

Peter was as well aware as Paul that there were many women in the early church who were faced with the sometimes almost unbearable problem of being married to an unsaved husband. To them, Peter's counsel was that they so conduct themselves in a spirit of genuine Christian grace that, even though their husbands might not like their spoken witness, they would still be convinced by the wives' godly conduct and turn to Christ. Peter's emphasis on quiet, consistent, Christian behavior, however strange it may sound to a modern "women's libber," is good advice, and many godly wives prove its validity every day.

COUNSEL TO HUSBANDS

Peter not only addressed wives but exhorted Christian husbands as well. He taught them to be considerate, thoughtful, and respectful of their wives. A husband should recognize his wife's femininity and understand that he needs his wife just as much as she needs him. It is in fact at this point that Peter stressed that they were "heirs with you. . . ."

There is a suggestion here that if a husband refused to treat his wife properly, he would not only impair a beautiful relationship but would displease the Lord. There is a spiritual dimension to marriage and, according to Peter, we run the risk of a hindered prayer life if we do not understand and accept this. Peter would agree with Paul that the measure of a man's spirituality is not his public profession but his integrity and considerateness in his home. "Husbands, in the same way be considerate as you live with your wives, and treat them with respect as the weaker partner and as heirs with you of the gracious gift of life, so that nothing will hinder your prayers" (1 Peter 3:7).

STUDY QUESTIONS

1. What is significant about the Apostle Peter's marriage?

2. What does Peter's story teach us about our attitude to "in-laws"? How can such relationships be improved?

3. How do you understand Peter's expression: "heirs with you of the gracious gift of life"?

4. What does Peter mean by "the unfading beauty of a gentle and quiet spirit"?

5. Under what circumstances is a "silent witness" more effective than a spoken one?

6. In what ways can Christian husbands show that they are considerate?

7. What things hinder family prayers?

PART FOUR

CONTEMPORARY APPLICATIONS

Oh grant us light, that we may know
The wisdom Thou alone canst give;
That truth may guide where'er we go
And virtue bless where'er we live.

Oh grant us light, that we may see
Where error lurks in human lore,
And turn our doubting minds to Thee,
And love Thy simple word the more.

Laurence Tuttiett
1825-97

CHAPTER FOURTEEN

THE BIBLE AND THE SINGLE PERSON

THE OLD TESTAMENT

The Old Testament has almost nothing to say on the subjects of celibacy and the single life. This is not surprising since marriage and family life were considered normal and desirable among the Hebrews. Not to marry and not to have family was almost a mark of divine displeasure.

It would be hard to base a brief for celibacy, even for spiritual leaders, on any teaching found in the Old Testament. We see that the prophets (with the notable exception of Jeremiah and Daniel), the priests, the Levites, the kings, the judges, and all others who bore office in Israel, were married and involved in regular family life. That their marriages were sometimes less than ideal, and that their families were not always exemplary, cannot be denied. However, despite the failures, celibacy was not taught as an alternative. This still held true in those cases where individuals were involved in strict, religious vows to live the "separate life." Witness the cases of the Nazirites and the Recabites (Numbers 6 and Jeremiah 35). The only conjugal limit on a priest was that he not marry a divorcee nor a prostitute (Leviticus 21:7). In the case of the high priest he was also prohibited from marrying a widow (Leviticus 21:13, 14; Ezekiel 44:22).

It was only with the development of community life, in groups like the Essene sect of the Jews, that celibacy came into vogue. Even the Essenes were divided on the issue, and while some undertook vows of celibacy, others did not. Marriage was practiced in the Qumran community despite its strong commitment to an austere, separated life-style.

In one Old Testament story, some unmarried women were able to take their full place in society and receive the family inheritance (Numbers 27:1-11). But even in this case, these women were later married within their own tribal group (Numbers 36:1-12). Then there is the rather unusual tale of Jephthah's daughter who, as a result of her father's rash vow, was never able to marry. In this instance we again see that the single state, far from being advocated, was considered inferior. Perpetual virginity was to be lamented (Judges 11:38).

OUR LORD'S TEACHING

We have already recognized that while Jesus approved marriage, he himself, like his forerunner John the Baptist, never married. His singleness was evidently necessary for the fulfillment of his unique, saving mission.

In our Lord's well-known teaching about marriage and divorce, he touched on the subject of celibacy: "Not everyone can accept this teaching, but only those to whom it has been given. For some are eunuchs because they were born that way; others were made that way by men; and others have renounced marriage because of the kingdom of heaven. The one who can accept this should accept it" (Matthew 19:11, 12).

In order to better understand Jesus' words here we must see them in context. He had just answered the Pharisee's test question about "grounds for divorce." Our Lord answered that marriage was instituted by God and ideally is to be dissolved by no man. His explanation about the Mosaic granting of a "bill of divorcement" was really aside from the main purpose of his reply.

It was in fact our Lord's insistence on the permanence of marriage that occasioned his disciples' ill-advised comment, "If this is the situation between a husband and wife it is better not to marry" (v. 10). One wonders if some of the disciples themselves were parties to unhappy marriages and secretly hoped Jesus might approve of their dissolving those marriages. If that was the case, then they were disappointed in Jesus' reply. Their words seem to convey the feeling that if there is no way out of an unhappy marriage situation, then better not get married in the first place.

Bearing this in mind, we get the drift of Jesus' reply. He certainly repudiated all such negative attitudes toward marriage. He recognized that there were some people who were unable to marry because of certain congenital defects, or because they had been sterilized. But these were exceptional cases. Then there were others who had decided, for their own reasons, that they might better serve God by renouncing marriage.

Jesus, although single himself, rejected his disciples' view. When he said, "the one who can accept this should accept it" (v. 12), he was not saying that if a person can accept celibacy, he should. Rather he was saying that a person should accept God's order in creation, which is, "one man for one woman." To regard marriage simply as a biological expedient or divorce as an easy option was unacceptable to Jesus. Such ideas totally deny God's purpose in the creation of male and female as complementary partners. If this was difficult for our Lord's disciples to accept then, it is much harder for many of us today. Many people appear to think of marriage in terms of an outmoded tradition, and have substituted their own easygoing divorce-on-demand, free-love ethic.

PAUL'S TEACHING

Paul's teaching on the single life is largely confined to 1 Corinthians 7. Since we have already dealt with this passage at some length in another context, we shall simply highlight one or two points. Before doing so we should note that Paul supported marriage and family life. Only under exceptional circumstances did he prefer the single state, and then, only in the context of the will of God and as a matter of personal choice. Paul nowhere legislated either marriage or celibacy, but generally tried to offer guidance to Christians to remain in the situation where they find themselves and to seek there to glorify God (1 Corinthians 7:20).

The verses most frequently quoted are: "I wish that all men were as I am. But each man has his own gift from God; one has this gift, another has that. Now to

the unmarried and widows I say: It is good for them
to stay unmarried, as I am. But if they cannot control
themselves, they should marry, for it is better to
marry than to burn with passion" (1 Corinthians
7:7-9).

At the time of this writing, Paul was obviously
unmarried. Whether he had been married and his
wife had died or deserted him has no bearing on
the main issue. The point is that Paul, himself
unattached, wished those who were unmarried would
remain so. Before examining his reasons for this
preference, let us recognize that the apostle saw
every Christian as responsible to the Lord for his own
life and testimony. He suggested that some were gifted
to remain celibate while others were gifted to marry.
Each must be fully persuaded in his own mind and
neither must seek to attempt to legislate for, nor foist
his opinions upon the other.

Coming to Paul's reasons, it is important to
recognize that his marriage ethic was conditioned by
the phrase "because of the present crisis" (v. 26).
Such was the situation in Corinth and such was
Paul's belief that if the Lord's return might be soon, it
would be better for single people to remain single.
Someone said, "He who marries and has children has
given hostages to fortune." In other words, because of
the very real possibility of Christians facing suffering
and persecution for Christ, Paul was implying that
the single person was exposing himself to more risk if
he married. It is hard enough to be tortured and
murdered, but to watch loved ones suffer and die
would be worse (v. 28).

Some have interpreted Paul as teaching that
marriage was simply a way to make sex relations
legal. They suggest that his phrase, "It is better to

marry than burn," represents a very low view of marriage and offers it as a second rate expedient. This is unfortunate and clearly misreads Paul's meaning. We shall understand this if we not only read this passage in context, but also if we examine Paul's teaching about marriage in Ephesians.

The words, "it is better to marry than to burn," clearly relate to the circumstances of Paul's original readers. They lived in the immoral city of Corinth where even prostitution was practiced in the name of religion, and where evil masqueraded as virtue. No doubt many of the Christian converts from paganism found the moral demands of the gospel rather stringent. There may also have been zealots in the Corinthian church who, like some of our contemporaries, believed and taught that sex was a dirty word, even within the proper boundaries of marriage. Paul was realistic enough to understand that, given these circumstances, it would be wise to set things straight. He therefore told his friends at Corinth, in answering specific questions, the wording of which is unknown to us, that there is more danger in repression than in expression. Given the prurient atmosphere of Corinth, it would be dangerous for anyone with normal sexual desires to refrain from proper marital relationships just because he supposed that this was a condition of salvation and membership in the Christian church.

Paul was not offering a "counsel of perfection," but was in fact giving sound advice to normal human beings with normal sex drives. Paul was against unbridled lust and extramarital experimentation. What he *was* for is *marriage*, especially if one is not spiritually called to the celibate life.

Later in this passage Paul gave his further reason

for advocating that unmarried people remain single. He wrote, "I would like you to be free from concern. An unmarried man is concerned about the Lord's affairs—how he can please the Lord. But a married man is concerned about the affairs of this world— how he can please his wife—and his interests are divided. An unmarried woman or virgin is concerned about the Lord's affairs: Her aim is to be devoted to the Lord in both body and spirit. But a married woman is concerned about the affairs of this world— how she can please her husband. I am saying this for your own good, not to restrict you, but that you live in a right way in undivided devotion to the Lord" (1 Corinthians 7:32-35).

Clearly we can have no quarrel with Paul's intent here. He is anxious that a Christian should have a right perspective on life and a true sense of values.

Paul believed that the end of the world was coming. His actual words were, "What I mean brothers, is that the time is short" (v. 29). Because the Second Advent was so close, he was suggesting that nothing should distract their attention, not even marriage.

This does not imply that because Paul's early expectations about Christ's return were not realized that his teaching is invalidated. It is simply pointing out the main thrust of his argument. Judged from the perspective of eternity, Paul's eschatology is vindicated, as is his advice. Christians can be so obsessed with the affairs of family life that they miss the whole point of their election by grace. A single person can be far more ambitious and world-centered than a married person who is responsible for a family. And for some, married life and family responsibility can be great incentives to godliness.

Being married can teach us how utterly dependent on God we are, not only for our personal survival but for that of loved ones. So while there is nothing intrinsically wrong with the single life, any thoughtful and honest person will admit that if one only has himself or herself to please, he or she is quite likely to do it. Conversely, if I am bound to consider other people and their happiness, I am less likely to end up like the "self-made man who worships his maker."

Neither the married person nor the unmarried person or single parent has any corner on devotion to Christ. The criterion of spirituality is not marital status but whether Jesus Christ is the Lord of our life.

In concluding this chapter we must do two things. On the one hand, we must reject the sad opinion of some misguided Christians. On the other, we must offer encouragement to other Christians who are now single.

The practice and advocacy of celibacy in the Christian church from the fourth century onward represents a denial of the teaching of Scripture. It might also be seen as a tendency to tolerate heretical opinions in order to accommodate pagan philosophy. It is sad that some of the teaching of the early church was tainted by dualism, the view that there is a kind of eternal separation between good and evil and that anything material tends to belong on the side of evil. It is a rehash of the ancient Greek idea that the spirit is good and the body is evil. The incarnation forever refutes that misconception.

It was this kind of confused thinking that led to monasticism, asceticism, and celibacy. It also suggested that marriage was a "second best." The names of famous Christians like Jerome, Augustine, and Ambrose are all cited in support of celibacy. Fortunately, with the Reformation and its return to biblical thinking, marriage came back into its own.

There is absolutely nothing wrong with being single. If someone is single because he has chosen to be so "for the sake of the kingdom," then we salute that person. On the other hand, someone may be single not by choice but because, though the person might wish it, the opportunity of marriage has not come. In this case, it is important to remember that if this is God's will at the present, then such a person is blessed with the opportunity to discover spiritual wholeness in the stewardship of time and freedom by serving others. Such persons should be encouraged in the knowledge that they stand in the company of such great people of the faith as Jeremiah, Daniel, Hananiah, Mishael, Azariah, John the Baptist, Mary, Martha, and probably Dorcas, Phoebe, and Paul.

Then there are those who are called to the difficult yet honored task of being single parents. These carry a special burden and certainly should expect the understanding and help of their brothers and sisters in Christ. It would be easy under these circumstances to become bitter and even suspicious of those who might offer to help. However, it is better that they recognize their need and seek God's grace not only to cope, but to grow through the experience. They have the responsibility of filling the role of two parents, and that may sometimes seem impossible. How they face the challenge will determine not only their children's chance to make it in life, but also their own wholeness in Christ.

STUDY QUESTIONS
1. What are the dangers of an overemphasis o
celibacy?
2. In what ways can a single person find fulfillm
3. What are some of the advantages of the single l
4. How can the Christian church best help one-
parent families?
5. What are areas of life in which single people
experience particular problems?
6. Suggest ways of dealing with worry and
frustration.

ꝛ C E

" 'I hate divorce,' says the Lord God of Israel" (Malachi
2:16). Divorce is one of the most vexing questions of
society today. It used to be a minor social problem,
and was almost never encountered within the
Christian church. Today, however we may feel about
it, divorce has reached epidemic proportions and has
invaded every kind of church and family. Once it
seemed easy to paint the issues in black and white.
That is no longer possible. Perhaps that is a good
thing because at least it sends us back to the Bible to
think carefully and prayerfully about the issues
involved.

THE OLD TESTAMENT
Apart from the above verse from Malachi, we find
very little about divorce in the Old Testament. There
are probably several reasons for this. First, the
Hebrews set great store by the family and sought to
guard it against breakdown. Second, the strong
teaching of the Jewish faith meant that anything

that tended toward moral laxity was frowned on or punished. Third, the society of Bible times was not affluent, and divorce is a social problem that is more common during periods of material affluence.

The only Old Testament passage which deals with the subject of divorce in any detail is: "If a man marries a woman who becomes displeasing to him because he finds something indecent about her, and he writes her a certificate of divorce, gives it to her and sends her from his house, and if after she leaves his house she becomes the wife of another man, and her second husband dislikes her and writes her a certificate of divorce, gives it to her and sends her from his house, or if he dies, then her first husband, who divorced her, is not allowed to marry her again after she has been defiled" (Deuteronomy 24:1-4).

However strange they may sound to modern ears, these words from the ancient Torah tell us two things. First, they show that such a thing as divorce was permitted in Israel. The New Testament will tell us that it was condoned only because of man's sinfulness (Matthew 19:8). Second, they show that divorce must be officially and judicially supervised. That is to say, there must be clear "grounds for divorce," called here, "something indecent." Divorce must never be undertaken frivolously nor arbitrarily.

The certificate of divorce was a safeguard against further injury and was not a permit for further license. It required a man to put his signature, and, indirectly, his reputation on the line. It insured that the wife he was dismissing be afforded due respect. Lacking such a document and its implied legal protection, life would have been unbearable if not dangerous for women, whether they were guilty or innocent.

This Mosaic legislation also shows that divorce was not only viewed as a complete dissolution of marriage but might be followed by remarriage, or even a third marriage. The only legal proviso was that the parties to a divorce might not remarry each other.

Herein lies the pathos of the Lord's challenge to Judah through the prophet Isaiah: "Where is your mother's certificate of divorce with which I sent her away?" (Isaiah 50:1). A similar note is struck in Jeremiah's prophecy: " 'If a man divorces his wife and she leaves him and marries another man should he return to her again? Would not the land be completely defiled? But you have lived as a prostitute with many lovers—would you now return to me?' declares the Lord" (Jeremiah 3:1).

The point of the prophet's message was that Judah, viewed metaphorically as God's wife (Isaiah 62; Ezekiel 16; Hosea 1:2), had been so flagrantly adulterous spiritually (idolatrous) that God divorced her. However, although according to the law a husband could not remarry his divorced wife, Jehovah still yearned over his estranged wife and was willing to welcome her back.

Divorce might also be involved when two people were not yet married but simply betrothed. Evidently betrothal was deemed to be as binding as marriage and could be legally dissolved only by divorce. The importance of betrothal is stressed in Deuteronomy 22:23 and 28 where a clear distinction is drawn between the rape of a "virgin pledged to be married," and that of a "virgin who is not pledged to be married." The man who raped the unbetrothed virgin was required to marry her and never allowed to divorce her. The man who violated the betrothed virgin was executed.

It is the possible divorce of a betrothed woman that is referred to in the story of Joseph and Mary (Matthew 1:18-21). Joseph, faced with Mary's unexplained pregnancy, thought about the compassionate alternative of divorce, until he was reassured by the angel of the Lord.

Two other passages complete the Old Testament teaching on divorce. One is in Deuteronomy 22:13-19, which has to do with a husband's slandering his wife. A wife who is falsely accused by her husband of premarital sex can never be divorced by him. The other has to do with priests in Israel, of whom we read: "They shall not marry women defiled by prostitution or divorced from their husbands." The regulations for the high priest were even more demanding: "The woman he marries must be a virgin. He must not marry a widow, a divorced woman, or a woman defiled by prostitution, but only a virgin from his own people" (Leviticus 21:14; Ezekiel 44:22).

JESUS' TEACHING
Our Lord's teaching on the subject of divorce occurs in two contexts. The first is in the sermon on the Mount: "It has been said, 'Anyone who divorces his wife must give her a certificate of divorce.' But I tell you that anyone who divorces his wife, except for marital unfaithfulness, causes her to commit adultery, and anyone who marries a woman so divorced commits adultery" (Matthew 5:31, 32).

The second is in his reply to the Pharisees who asked, "Is it lawful for a man to divorce his wife for any and every reason?" In this instance Jesus replied: "Moses permitted you to divorce your wives because your hearts were hard. But it was not this way from the beginning. I tell you that anyone who divorces his wife, except for marital unfaithfulness, and marries another woman commits adultery" (Matthew 19:3, 8, 9).

In these words Jesus was stating the principle that divorce was not to be treated as an easy escape route from marriage. The certificate of divorce was not the important thing, as if by waving a piece of paper a man could dissolve his marriage and at the same time salve his conscience. The important matter was why the man divorced his wife. If his grounds were other than "marital unfaithfulness," then his issuing of a divorce document was like issuing a license for immorality, since the first marriage still stood, at least in the eyes of the law and of God.

The Lord reinforced this in Matthew 19:3-12 by adding another dimension. Once again he was approving the Mosaic law but pointed out that the issue of the divorce certificate was an accommodation which had developed because of the hardness of the human heart. The Pharisees wanted a "for any and every cause" type of divorce law. Jesus not only repudiated such a suggestion but limited divorce to the marriage that had already been spoiled by unfaithfulness. Jesus was not issuing a permit for divorce but putting a limit on it. As far as he was concerned, divorce, like sin, was an intruder. It was not part of God's plan for man nor ever could be (Matthew 19:4, 5).

The question is often asked whether Jesus' words permitted the remarriage of a divorced person. Quite opposite answers have been given by Bible scholars. It seems that while Jesus' words do nothing to encourage the remarriage of divorced persons, they may under certain circumstances permit it. After all, the divorce itself is not "committing adultery" as some people suggest.

Jesus' point was that to issue a certificate of divorce for the wrong reasons may cause a person to commit adultery by cohabiting with another than one's spouse. If a person's mate is guilty of marital unfaithfulness, let it be understood that he is not required to divorce, nor is this his only option. If such a person marries someone else, then it would seem, on the basis of Jesus' words, that neither the man nor his new partner has committed adultery.

PAUL'S TEACHING

"To the married I give this command (not I, but the Lord): A wife must not separate from her husband. But if she does, she must remain unmarried or else be reconciled to her husband. And a husband must not divorce his wife.

"To the rest I say this (I, not the Lord): if any brother has a wife who is not a believer and she is willing to live with him, he must not divorce her. And if a woman has a husband who is not a believer and he is willing to live with her, she must not divorce him. . . . But if the unbeliever leaves, let him do so. A believing man or woman is not bound in such circumstances: God has called us to live in peace" (1 Corinthians 7:10-15).

It is important to read Paul's teaching about divorce in its context, here in 1 Corinthians 7. For Paul, as for his Master, the ideal was the permanent and faithful union of husband and wife (Romans 7:1-3; Ephesians 5:31; 1 Corinthians 7:39). However, he, like Christ and like Moses, understood only too well that hardened, sinful hearts had distorted God's patterns.

Here in 1 Corinthians 7, Paul's basic advice was that Christians remain in the situation in which they find themselves. Their Christianity must not be used as an excuse for disrupting either social or family relationships (1 Corinthians 7:17-24). Furthermore, Paul accepted marriage whether contracted by Christians before or after they were converted to Christ, and whether in front of pagan or Christian authorities. It is doubtful whether in Paul's day there were church weddings in our modern sense.

A careful reading of Paul's teaching on divorce suggests that he was consistently in agreement with Christ. He did not allow a Christian to divorce his partner (vv. 10, 11), unless, of course, it was for the reason stated by Jesus. He also taught that if a Christian is divorced by a non-Christian partner, then that Christian is released from his or her marriage bond and is free to marry someone else (v. 15). Of course, Paul was writing to a given set of circumstances, in which a pagan, perhaps angered by his wife's conversion to Christ, had decided to divorce her. In this situation Paul, as an inspired apostle and having the mind of Christ, regarded such desertion as final, as in the same category as marital unfaithfulness. Again, Paul did not recommend remarriage, nor did he see it as inevitable. In fact, the slighted Christian spouse could choose to remain single and with Christlike compassion and mercy continue to pray for her former spouse (v. 16). Such an attitude could only amaze and be admired by onlookers.

We see then that what the Bible teaches on divorce is brief, and in the light of the contemporary scene,

seems to leave many unanswered questions.
However, the general principles are clear. It is for the Christian reader to seek "through endurance and the encouragement of the Scriptures" not only to find hope, but wisdom (Romans 15:4). There are very few situations that cannot be satisfactorily resolved through these means, and through the supporting fellowship and resources of the Christian community. In any event let us remember that the Bible nowhere suggests that divorce is the unpardonable sin, even if initiated for the wrong reasons.

STUDY QUESTIONS

1. Why are there so many divorces today?
2. Consider the implications of the Old Testament's permitting remarriage after divorce.
3. What do the Old Testament laws about the marital status of priests (Leviticus 21:7, 14) suggest about Christian leaders and divorce?
4. How do you understand Malachi 2:16?
5. Are we right in assuming that Jesus' "excepting clause" implies that remarriage after divorce is permissible?
6. Does Paul's teaching about marriage in 1 Corinthians 7 allow for the possibility of divorce?
7. Why do you think the church forgives other sins much more readily than divorce?
8. How can we help young people safeguard against divorce?
9. Is there sometimes an innocent party in divorce?
10. What is God's ideal regarding marriage?

HOW CAN FAMILIES SURVIVE?

We have tried to resist the temptation to write yet another book of advice on marriage and family. Instead we have attempted to ask and answer the question: "What saith the Scriptures?" The measure of our failure or success must be whether the book has illuminated or obscured divine truths.

"Can the family survive?" is a question that some feel is now open to debate. When we look at today's problems, we can understand their skepticism. However, in the light of Scripture we share Paul's optimism. As he stood on the wave-swept deck of a sinking ship he cried out, "So keep up your courage, men, for I have faith in God that it will happen just as he told me" (Acts 27:25). We must believe that the family can and will survive. Our present interest is in "how." Six principles can insure family survival and success.

1. RECOGNIZE THE SPIRITUAL SIGNIFICANCE OF THE FAMILY

The family is not a phenomenon of social evolution but the result of God's design. It was conceived not in the mind of man but in the loving heart of the eternal God. The family is significant for many reasons, and not least of these is that it is a revelation of God.

As we have seen, man was made in the image and likeness of God. This means that if we want to know what God is like, one place to begin is to look at man in his complementary aspects of male and female and in the context of family. Granted, the "image of God" has been defaced by sin, but behind the defacement there is still authentic currency. The Bible has a beautiful expression to describe humanity: "You made him a little lower than the heavenly beings and crowned him with glory and honor" (Psalm 8:5).

Affronted by man's sin, how easy it would have been for God to destroy or disable him. Evidently God had something else in mind. Instead of destroying man, God blessed him, preserved his significance, and allowed him the joys of family life. Indeed he went much further than that in grace, and so provided for man's rescue and reinstatement that one day God "became flesh and dwelt among us." He came not as a blinding light, condemning and forbidding, but as a human babe, the son of Mary, and an integral part of our human family. Here was no superman incubating from some stranded asteroid, but God manifest in flesh. Does this not give our race and our families significance?

But there is more here. The family is a revelation about the essential nature of God. For example, our experiences of relationship and society are only a small reflection of the society that is in the Godhead.

147

While the Bible teaches monotheism, its concept of God is trinitarian. Father, Son, and Holy Spirit are distinct in their persons, yet indivisible in their substance. In marriage we speak of two being one flesh. In Christian theology we speak of three persons being one God. Granted there are great differences and in some ways the comparison is hard to explain. Yet one thing is clear. Just as there is relationship in marriage and family, so is there in God. God's words have great meaning: "Let us make man in our image, in our likeness" (Genesis 1:26). The plural number of the verb and pronouns here is clearly important and reminds us that our diverse genders and our real relationships reflect our ultimate source and Creator. To dismiss these terms simply as "royal plurals" is poor exegesis, particularly in the light of the scrupulous monotheism of the Hebrew Scriptures.

Further, just as there is society in the Godhead so is there family. Without doubt, the Fatherhood of God and the Sonship of Christ are unique, but these concepts of biblical theology are more than mere anthropomorphisms. We have already noticed that it was in the teaching of our Lord that the divine Fatherhood was specially revealed. It is to Jesus that we owe our understanding that he stood in unique relation to God, as Son to Father. In his humanity he said, "The Father is greater than I" (John 14:28); but in his deity he said, "I and the Father are one" (John 10:30). The first of these two expressions is as much a claim to deity as is the second, since only God can compare himself with God. In case anyone doubts the implication of the words: "I and the Father are one," we should note the Jews' immediate interpretation of them: "You, a mere man, claim to be God" (John 10:25-36).

As important as these theological truths may be, we are not here so much concerned with them as with the relationship of Father and Son in the Godhead. Although we have noted this elsewhere, it is worth repeating that despite the widely held supposition that our belief in divine Fatherhood is a projection of our innate father-consciousness, Paul said precisely the opposite in Ephesians 3:15. Certainly our appreciation of God's Fatherhood is colored by our experience in our human family; but that is vastly different from saying that we think of God only in terms of "Father" because we seek instinctively to allay our sense of lostness and foster our desire for spiritual security and paternity. The truth is that when we call God "Father" we call him by his name. Inscrutable though it may seem, there is family in God. In fact, in Genesis there is a metaphor that hints of the motherhood in God. According to some scholars, Genesis 1:2 could be translated "the Spirit of God was *brooding* upon the face of the deep."

Of course we are much more familiar with the New Testament idea that there is a mystical sense in which the Church stands in relation to Christ as a bride to her husband. Again this is a development from the Old Testament picture of Israel as the wife of Jehovah (Isaiah 62:4, 5). We must be careful not to read too much into this, but at least it is saying that human relationships have their archetypes in God.

Add to these concepts the biblical teaching about God's love, providence, and authority and how these divine attributes parallel our family responsibilities, and we begin to see how important our human relationships are. It is not saying too much to insist that in our humanity, in our sexuality, in our relationships, in our marriages, and in our families we can learn something about God. Practically speaking this means that in our society, which is generally blind and closed to divine revelation, a Christian family may very well become an eloquent message about God and a witness to his nature.

2. PLAY IT BY THE RULES

Another key to success in family living is to "play it by the rules." This is not to imply that marriage and family are games, although many of our contemporaries seem to think so, judging from their life-style. Nor are we suggesting that slavish adherence to a book of rules guarantees success. What we are saying is that the safest, happiest way to order our lives is in the clear light of the Word of God. The Psalmist said, "It is he that made us and not we ourselves" (Psalm 100:3). It surely follows that since our Maker knows how we function best we are wise to live in accordance with his "operating manual." There is no question that we can opt to cheat, change the rules, or improvise, but to do so is to invite trouble.

The Bible is like the book which is enclosed with all new appliances. It is usually called "the manufacturer's instructions." Unfortunately, many people upon purchasing their new gadget immediately burn the instructions with the wrappings, then wonder why things do not work right. So it is in life and family. All too many of us forge ahead as if we by nature knew all the answers. We rarely if ever consult the Maker's Manual, the Bible. Is it surprising then that so many marriages, homes, families, and lives are wrecked? After all, the God who made us and who invented family has certainly not left us without guidelines for our happiness and success. We ask for problems when we ignore them.

As we consult God's Word we discover not only a clear set of instructions, rules, and examples, but a secure ground for authority in life and home. The Bible is full of real family examples. It tells us about the meaning and therefore the sanctity and permanence of marriage. There are clear words about our roles, responsibilities, and relationships. It speaks to husbands, wives, fathers, mothers, single people, children, and even grandparents.

God's rules, we should remember, come with the built-in strength to observe them. It is rather like one of the modern varieties of "instant cameras." The first models required fully charged batteries. Everything worked well and the pictures were properly exposed, providing the camera's battery was fresh. But that was the snag. People let the batteries go dead and then, after complaining about its inefficiency, discarded the camera. The manufacturer overcame the problem brilliantly. He built the energizer into the film. This meant that the successful picture no longer depended on the camera but on the film. The power was built in. So it is in a sense with the Bible. It is not simply a dead book of rules but the living—or, better, "life-giving"—Word of God. The same Holy Spirit who indwells the Christian inspires the sacred page of Scripture. He is not only its original Author but its continuing Author. As we read Scripture we are not only *told* how to run our lives and families— if we respond in faith, we are given the strength to do it!

3. PRACTICE CONSISTENT CHRISTIANITY

In this the third of our "keys to family success," we must "practice what we preach," to use the Apostle James' idea. Many people suppose that because they marry in church, say "grace" at mealtime, maintain a family altar, tithe their income, and do other religious things, that theirs is a Christian home. However, there is much more to it than that. The words of Moses, which we have considered in another context, put it well: "These commandments that I give you today are to be upon your hearts. Impress them on your children. Talk about them when you sit at home and when you walk along the road, when you lie down and when you get up" (Deuteronomy 6:6, 7).

What these words tell us is that no area of a Christian family life is secular or profane, but that each is sacred. In a Christian marriage or family, as in an individual Christian life, Jesus Christ must be acknowledged and obeyed as Lord. All relationships, all decisions, and all activities will be open to the scrutiny of God. Roles will be accepted, not grudgingly as if we are afraid of losing face, but happily, as a part of our intelligent worship. Husbands will exercise leadership in love; wives will submit and support their husbands; parents will nurture their children in grace; and children will obey their parents in the Lord.

In a home where Jesus Christ is Lord there will be a sacrificial love, transparent honesty, good communication, the proper exercise of discipline, the gentle art of being considerate, practical Christian concern, unselfishness, trust, and a willingness to forgive.

4. ACCEPT RESPONSIBLE INVOLVEMENT

A family, unlike a chain, is stronger than its weakest link and amazingly resilient. In some special sense, it is more than the sum of its many members. There is a kind of corporate identity or ethos about a family and this can be a great resource of strength and encouragement. However, only when each member accepts his responsibility does the family function at its best. In this context we may not be far wrong to suggest that a family is not so much a corporation with its various levels of administration but a co-op in which all participate, contribute, and benefit.

In the Christian family, practically speaking, everyone contributes—time, love, and material support. Everyone must accept household responsibilities, not as demeaning or undesirable chores, but as opportunities for loving service. Children and young people must be trained to accept responsibility. The Bible reminds us that it is a good thing for a young person "to bear the yoke in youth" (Lamentations 3:27).

There is likely to be much more involvement in the extended family than in the nuclear family. However, even where there is simply Father, Mother, Johnny, and Mary—each one can play a vital role. There is no better family therapy, call it "glue" if you will, than total participation. Whether it is a football game, a picnic, a holiday, or things much more mundane like cleaning the house or weeding the lawn, no one should be allowed to use the excuse of being "too busy," not even Dad! Conversely, Mother should not be expected to carry the heavy end while others get off scot-free.

Children grow up poor indeed, and practically handicapped, if they are not told and shown how to do things and allowed to do them. A son whose father teaches him simple plumbing or management will always be grateful that Dad "took the time." A daughter, and certainly her future husband, will always be glad that Mother taught her cooking and similar basics. Parents do their children a disservice by waiting on them, just as they do when they regularly hire baby-sitters.

5. CULTIVATE A STRONG ASSOCIATION WITH A CHURCH

While Scripture teaches the primacy of the family, it usually views the family in the context of the church. And of course this works both ways. The local church, made up of families, relies on them for service and support. The strength of a Christian church is related not only to the spirituality of its members but to the strength of its families. Conversely, the family, as Martin Luther suggested, is "the school of the Christian life." In our families we learn about rule, order, covenant, commitment, discipline, obedience, and love. All these factors are important and we bring them into our church life.

We have seen in our studies not only how important the home is in relation to the church, but also that the Scriptures make a man's response to family responsibility the criterion of his qualification for church leadership.

There are many ways in which Christian families can support their churches. They will try to attend as many of the public services as possible, always remembering that such attendance must not be allowed to impair the life of the family. A family can help its church through prayer, giving, witness in the community, respect for leaders, hospitality, and sundry other services. A further area of meaningful involvement is in church families standing together and helping each other.

6. RENEW YOUR CONFIDENCE IN GOD

This key to family success is probably the most important of all. It reminds us that whether we are single or married, parents or children, we can only live responsibly and make our mark for God if we have confidence in him. While, as we have observed, the New Testament speaks about household salvation, it nowhere suggests that becoming a Christian depends on our heredity or is guaranteed by our family association. Unless we personally receive Jesus Christ to be our Lord and Savior, our Christian heritage, like our parents' faith, may be as much a liability to us in the Day of Judgment as an asset. In some ways it is better not to have known the truth at all than to have known it and witnessed its reality and power in our home, and still to have rejected it!

Having trusted Christ for salvation we had better learn to trust him for everything else. Whatever we have, we simply hold in trust for God. We must ever beware of the danger of forgetting God when we are full (Deuteronomy 6:10-12). The wealthy family is in much greater spiritual danger than the poor one. Material things have ruined many more homes, families, and children than has poverty—not that there is any virtue in poverty. It is simply a matter of fact that the more dependent we are on God, the more we shall draw on his resources and enjoy them. Children learn unforgettable lessons about God's grace and provision when they observe, firsthand, God meeting their family's needs. Christian parents had far better forego financial and social advancement than the enjoyment of ordinary and simple pleasures with their children.

We end on a confident note. Let us trust God for our family and for our children. When Paul answered the jailer's urgent question in the prison cell at Philippi, he said, "Believe in the Lord Jesus, and you will be saved—you and your household" (Acts 16:31).

What Paul meant is clear. On the one hand, salvation is intensely personal. God has no spiritual grandchildren. On the other, parents may very well trust God to save their children and pray to that end. In this matter as in so many others: we have not because we ask not; or, if we ask, we do not ask in faith (James 1:6-8; 4:2). Praise God for all who, like Timothy, can give thanks for generations of believing parents and grandparents.

APPENDIXES

LEARNING FROM BIBLE FAMILIES

OLD TESTAMENT

Family	Reference	Situation	Lessons, Observations, and Warnings
1. Noah, his wife, three sons, and three daughters-in-law	Genesis 5-9	Lived in the corrupt antediluvian society.	Trusted in God and expressed faith in action. Saved, blessed, and brought into covenant relationship with God. Family broken up due to the tragic effect of drunkenness.
2. Abraham, his wife Sarah, and son Isaac, his wife's maid, Hagar, and her son Ishmael	Genesis 12-25	Called from paganism into a unique covenant relationship with God: Abraham known as "friend of God."	A husband and wife who rejected idolatry and materialism for a life of faith. Trusted God even in most trying circumstances. Willingly dedicated their child to God. Passed on a wonderful heritage to following generations. This story also warns against trying to do right things in the wrong way, and causing the family untold grief.
3. Lot, his wife, and two daughters	Genesis 12-19	A nomadic chief, nephew of Abraham; unfortunately had more money than sense.	A husband and wife who were prepared to compromise everything for wealth and prestige. Covetousness killed the mother. Drunkenness led the father to commit incest with his two daughters. Here is a striking warning to any family that puts gold before God.

Family	Reference	Situation	Lessons, Observations, and Warnings
4. Isaac and Rebekah, and their sons Esau, and Jacob	Genesis 22-28	Abraham's famous son and daughter-in-law.	A beautiful love story that ended sadly because once the couple married and became parents, they showed favoritism in their family and refused to exercise godly discipline.
5. Jacob	Genesis 25-49	Founder of the twelve tribes of Israel. Grandson of Abraham and brother of Esau.	A large family in which every human characteristic seemed to be represented. Polygamy caused family strife and jealousy. Not much evidence of discipline or family feeling. Dishonesty evidently undermined family trust and loyalty.
6. Joseph, Asenath and sons, Manasseh and Ephraim	Genesis 37-50	The son of Jacob who became a ruler in Egypt.	Although placed in a difficult situation, Joseph was a model of purity. An unfortunate family feud led ultimately to national division, showing how family problems can have wide repercussions.
7. Moses	Exodus 2	A family that triumphed over the problems created by slavery, racial oppression, and poverty.	Amram and Jochebed, Moses' parents, are models for all parents who would trust God for their families against great odds. Here was a mother who displayed great courage and risked everything to teach her children about God and the importance of true values in life.

Family	Reference	Situation	Lessons, Observations, and Warnings
8. Joshua and his family	Joshua 24:15	The occasion of the renewing of the covenant at Shechem, subsequent to the conquest of Canaan.	Joshua and his household are examples to all who are willing to declare their family loyalty to God even if other so-called believers are vacillating. This family's motto has been a challenge and blessing to many ever since.
9. Samson and his parents	Judges 13	The time of the Judges, when the Philistines were attacking Israel.	Here are parents who, although believers themselves, failed to communicate their spiritual values and moral standards to their son. They appear to have been too indulgent and mistook spoiling for kindness.
10. Boaz, Ruth, and Naomi	Ruth	A time of famine and recovery in the area of Bethlehem.	This is the story of a family that experienced hard times and considerable misunderstanding. Despite the problems, they trusted in the Lord and became a blessing to a whole community. Here is an example of a particularly happy in-law relationship.
11. Hannah, Elkanah, and their son Samuel	1 Samuel 1	A time of spiritual apathy, if not of national anarchy.	Here is a mother who, despite very difficult domestic circumstances which were aggravated by a polygamous husband, kept on praying. God not only answered her prayer and gave her a famous son, Samuel, but gave her strength and joy to cope. Her shining faith and commitment to God were a rebuke to the hollow sham of the religious pretenders around her.

Family	Reference	Situation	Lessons, Observations, and Warnings
12. Eli and Sons	1 Samuel 1-2	Same situation as above.	Eli is a warning to all religious fathers, particularly ministers and church leaders who are so busy in their "church" that they neglect their family. Although orthodox in faith and practice. here was a man who was spiritually backslidden and as a result helped his family on to ruin.
13. David and family	1 & 2 Samuel	The early days of the monarchy in Israel.	Although famous for his feats and conquests, David was a poor father. His several marriages and strong passions brought grief on himself and his family. He failed to discipline his children and reaped a dreadful harvest.
14. The Shu-nammite	2 Kings 4	The period of the divided kingdom.	This is the story of a godly woman who practiced the art of hospitality. She appears to have had more spiritual discernment than her husband. When her only son was stricken she knew instinctively to turn to the Lord and cast her burden upon him.
15. Job's family	Job 1	This story takes place in the land of Uz, probably in patriarchal times.	Job is an example to all fathers. He not only spent time with his children but was deeply concerned for their spiritual well-being. He experienced terrible suffering and bereavement but kept his faith in God. He was one of few men who could handle prosperity and adversity with equanimity.

Family	Reference	Situation	Lessons, Observations, and Warnings
16. The Virtuous Woman and her family	Proverbs 31	A poem by King Lemuel, in praise of womanhood.	Here is an exemplary wife and mother. She is praised for her industry, wisdom, and careful speech. She supports her husband's decisions and regards domestic responsibilities and motherhood as a noble calling from the Lord.
17. Isaiah, his wife and sons	Isaiah 8	The scene is set in Jerusalem in the time of King Ahaz, eighth century B.C.	Isaiah, his wife, and sons are a living witness to the nation of Judah that God can be trusted. His children evidently stood with him and shared his faith in God in a time of spiritual apostasy.
18. Hosea, his wife and children	Hosea	Probably contemporary with Jeremiah, prophecied particularly to the Northern Kingdom.	Hosea experienced the special heartache of an unfaithful partner. Although his heart was broken and he carried the additional responsibilities falling on a single parent, he maintained his trust in God. His life was in fact an acted parable about God's unfailing love for a faithless nation.

Family	Reference	Situation	Lessons, Observations, and Warnings

NEW TESTAMENT

Family	Reference	Situation	Lessons, Observations, and Warnings
19. Joseph, Mary, Jesus, and his brothers and sisters	Matthew 1-2; Luke 1-2	The period of the Roman occupation of Palestine when the Herods ruled as vassal kings in Judah.	Here is the wonderful story of how God deigned to express himself in the context of a human family. Joseph and Mary are ordinary people who accepted the regular routines of daily work and family life. The story of Jesus' obedience and submission to Joseph and his mother, Mary, is an example to all young people. There were misunderstandings even in this family, but Jesus handled them without resentment. Clearly there was love in this family.
20. Zacharias, Elizabeth, and John	Luke 1	Palestine during the reign of the Roman Emperor Augustus. Zacharias and Elizabeth lived near Jerusalem where he served as a temple priest.	Here were two older parents who accepted their son as a gift from God. They prepared themselves for his birth and accepted the responsibility of bringing him up for God. Although evidently living in modest circumstances, they were content and made a mark for God.

Family	Reference	Situation	Lessons, Observations, and Warnings
21. Mary, Martha, and Lazarus	Luke 10:38-42; John 11	Lived in Bethany near Jerusalem and evidently owned a nice home there.	This is the story of a brother and his two sisters who lived very happily together despite their different temperaments. Given to hospitality, they often had the privilege of entertaining Jesus in their home. They had learned to bring their problems to Jesus.
22. Mary and her son John Mark	Acts 12:12-17	Lived in a comfortable home in Jerusalem in the time of the early church. Mary was probably from Cyprus originally, and belonged to a priestly family.	Mary is an example to all women who have survived widowhood. She evidently busied herself in Christian work, made her home available to the Christians, and instructed her son in the ways of the Lord.
23. Priscilla and Aquila	Acts 18:2, 26; Romans 16:3; 1 Corinthians 16:19	They lived during the reign of Claudius and traveled in business ventures to various cities of the day.	A husband and wife who exemplified the grace of hospitality. Apparently childless, they not only worked hard at their trade of tentmaking, but took time to help others whenever possible. They were evidently good Bible students and enjoyed discipling others.

Family	Reference	Situation	Lessons, Observations, and Warnings
24. Philemon and family	Philemon	Lived at Colosse, probably about the middle of the first century.	Although apparently well-to-do, they used their resources for the Lord. They were very hospitable and their home was the meeting place for the Christian church in Colosse. Paul felt quite at home with them.
25. Lois, Eunice, and Timothy	Acts 16:1,2; 2 Timothy 1:5	Family lived at Ephesus during time of early church.	This story stresses the importance of one generation communicating its faith to the next: Lois, a grandmother who prayed; and Eunice, a mother who taught her son the Scripture. We see here the great influence women can have by responsibly accepting and fulfilling their domestic and family responsibilities.
26. House of Onesiphorus	2 Timothy 1:16, 17	Set in the city of Rome, probably A.D. 60.	This family is an example to all who seek to relieve the difficulties and distress of others. They were exemplary in their courage and determination.

A P P E N D I X   T W O
• •
A STUDY OUTLINE ON THE BIBLE AND MARRIAGE

1. MARRIAGE
Genesis 1:27; 2:18-
25; 3:6, 7; 3:21;
4:19; 6:1; 12:1-20;
20:2-4; 24:4, 51-
53, 57, 58, 67;
25:1; 26:7-11;
27:46; 28:1, 2;
29:18-30; 31:14;
34:12-14
Exodus 21:10;
21:3, 4; 22:16, 17
Leviticus 18:1-23;
21:13
Numbers 5:5-31
Deuteronomy 20:7;
24:1-4; 25:5-10
Ruth 4:5-10;
1 Samuel 1:2;
1 Kings 11:3-6
Proverbs 12:4; 18:22;
19:14
Isaiah 4:1; 62:4, 5
Hosea 1:2
Malachi 2:16
Matthew 1:25; 2:13,
14, 20; 5:31, 32;
19:2-9; 22:23-30
Luke 16:18
John 2:1-11
Romans 7:1-3
1 Corinthians 7:2-5,
9, 10-17, 27, 39,
40; 9:5; 11:11, 12
2 Corinthians 6:14
Ephesians 5:22, 33
1 Timothy 3:2, 12;
5:14; 4:1-3

Titus 2:4, 5
Revelation 19:7, 8

2. LIMITS REGARDING MARRIAGE
Exodus 34:15, 16
Leviticus 18:1-23;
20:10-14; 20:20,
21
Judges 14:3
1 Kings 11:2
Ezra 9:1, 2; 10:18-44
Nehemiah 13:23-28
1 Corinthians 7

3. SEXUAL PURITY REQUIRED
Exodus 20:14; 22:19
Leviticus 20:14-20
Deuteronomy 5:18;
22:13-30; 27:20-
23
Job 31:1
Matthew 5:27, 28;
19:18
John 8:1-11
1 Corinthians 5:1-5,
11
Galatians 5:19
1 Thessalonians 4:3

4. THE SINGLE LIFE
Psalm 68:6
Isaiah 54:4, 5
Isaiah 56:3-5
Jeremiah 16:2

Matthew 19:12
1 Corinthians 7:7, 8,
25, 26, 32-34
Revelation 14:4

5. FAMILY
Genesis 1:28; 4:1;
9:1, 7; 12:1; 17:7-
15; 18:19; 31:43;
33:2-5; 35:23-26
Exodus 12:3, 24-27;
13:14; 18:5
Leviticus 25:48, 49
Numbers 27:1-11;
36:1-9
Deuteronomy 21:1-15
Joshua 24:15
Ruth 4:5-10
2 Chronicles 20:13
Nehemiah 12:43
Job 1:1-5
Psalms 68:6; 113:9;
127:3-5; 128:3
Proverbs 13:22; 17:6
Isaiah 8:18
Matthew 10:34-37;
12:46-50; 13:55-
57; 19:29; 21:28-
31
Luke 1:5-7; 1:57-59;
15:21-32
John 19:25-27
Acts 16:30-34; 18:8;
23:16
Romans 16:7
1 Corinthians 1:16;
16:15

Galatians 4:1-7, 22, 23
Ephesians 5:22—6:4
1 Timothy 3:1-5, 8-12
2 Timothy 1:5
Philemon 2
Hebrews 12:7-11

6. GENEALOGICAL TABLES

Genesis 4:16-22; 5:3-32; 10:1-32; 11:10-32; 22:20-24; 25:1-4, 12-16; 35:22-26; 36:1-43
Exodus 6:14-25
Numbers 1—4; 26:1-65
Ruth 4:18-22
1 Chronicles 1—9
Ezra 7:1-5; 8:1-14
Matthew 1:1-17
Luke 3:23-38

7. HUSBANDS

Psalm 128:3
Proverbs 5:15-19; 18:22
Ecclesiastes 9:9
1 Corinthians 7:1-4, 14-16; 11:3
Ephesians 5:23, 25, 28-33
Colossians 3:19
1 Timothy 3:1-12; 5:8
1 Peter 3:7

8. WIVES

Genesis 3:16
Esther 1:20
Psalm 128:3
Proverbs 12:4; 19:14; 31:10-28

1 Corinthians 7:3, 4; 11:3
Ephesians 5:22-24, 33
Colossians 3:18
1 Timothy 3:11; 5:14
Titus 2:4, 5
1 Peter 3:1-6

9. PARENTS

Exodus 13:8, 14
Deuteronomy 4:9, 10; 6:7-9; 11:19, 20
Joshua 24:15
1 Kings 2:4
Psalm 78:3-8; 103:17, 18
Proverbs 22:6, 15; 23:13, 14
Isaiah 8:18; 54:13
Matthew 7:9-11; 18:3-5, 10; 19:14; 20:20, 21
1 Corinthians 7:14
Ephesians 6:4
Colossians 3:21
2 Timothy 3:15
Hebrews 12:7-11

10. CHILDREN

Genesis 4:1; 7:1, 13; 9:18; 17:19, 20; 21:1-6; 25:21-23; 27:25-29; 30:1; 31:16, 17; 37:3; 48:14-20
Exodus 2:1, 2; 11:5; 12:29; 13:1, 2; 21:22
Leviticus 12:1-8; 20:1, 2
Numbers 18:14-16
Deuteronomy 21:18-21

Joshua 4:21, 22; 24:15
1 Samuel 1:27, 28; 3:13
Matthew 18:2-6; 19:13-15; 21:16
Luke 1:13-15; 2:21-52; 9:47, 48
1 Corinthians 7:14
Galatians 4:19
Hebrews 12:5
1 John 3:1

11. CHILDREN'S RESPONSIBILITIES

Exodus 20:12; 21:15, 17
Leviticus 19:3
Deuteronomy 5:16; 27:16
Proverbs 1:8; 4:1; 6:20; 10:1; 13:1; 15:5; 23:22
Matthew 15:4-6; 19:19
Mark 7:9-13
Luke 2:51
Ephesians 6:1-3
Colossians 3:20
1 Timothy 5:4
Hebrews 12:7-11

12. DIVORCE

Leviticus 21:7, 14
Deuteronomy 24:1-4
Isaiah 50:1
Jeremiah 3:8
Ezekiel 44:22
Malachi 2:16
Matthew 1:19; 5:31, 32; 19:3-12
Mark 10:2-12
1 Corinthians 7:10-15

SCRIPTURE INDEX

29:14-30 21, 166
29:32-34 31
29:57, 58 21
30:1 167
30:2 31
30:6 31
30:22, 23 31
31:14 21, 166
31:16, 17 167
31:43 166
33:2-5 166
33:5 31
34:14 25
34:12-14 166
35:22-26 166, 167
36:1-43 167
37 35
37:3, 4 35, 167
48:14-20 167
48:15-22 34
49 34
49:3 34

Exodus
2 33
2:1, 2 167
4:22 36, 71
6:14-27 167
11 36
12:3, 24-27 166, 167
12:25-27 39
12:29 167
13:1, 2 167
13:2-12 64
13:8, 14 39, 167
13:12, 13 36
13:14 166, 167
18:5 166
20:12 40, 167
20:14 16, 166
21:3, 4 166
21:10 166
21:15, 17 42, 167
21:22 167
22:16, 17 166

22:19 166
34:15, 16 26, 166

Leviticus
12:1-8 167
12:3 64
12:3-8 32
12:4 64
12:8 64
18:1-23 166
18:7-17 26
18:20 23
18:22 16
19:3 167
20:1, 2 167
20:9 42
20:10-14 166
20:14-20 166
20:21 166
21:7-14 129, 145, 166, 167
21:14 43, 141
25:48, 49 166

Numbers
1-4 167
3:40-51 36
5:5-31 166
6 129
18:14-16 167
18:24 43
26:1-65 167
26:59 26
27:1-11 44, 129, 166
36:1-12 129, 166

Deuteronomy
4:9, 10 167
5:16 114, 167
5:18 166
6:4-7 38
6:6-9 152, 167
6:10-12 155
7:3, 4 26

Scripture Index